GENERATIONS
Phonics

GENERATIONS
Phonics

VOLUME 2

R.A. Sheats

Preface by Kevin Swanson

Generations
PASSING ON THE FAITH

Cover Artwork: Cedric Hohnstadt
Cover Design: Justin Turley
Interior Layout Design: Justin Turley and Sarah Lee Bryant

Published by:
Generations
19039 Plaza Drive Ste 210
Parker, Colorado 80134
www.generations.org

For more information on this and
other titles from Generations,
visit www.generations.org or call (888) 389-9080.

Dolch Sight Words by Grade

Pre-Primer		Primer		First Grade	
a	look	all	out	after	let
and	make	am	please	again	live
away	me	are	pretty	an	may
big	my	at	ran	any	of
blue	not	ate	ride	as	old
can	one	be	saw	ask	once
come	play	black	say	by	open
down	red	brown	she	could	over
find	run	but	so	every	put
for	said	came	soon	fly	round
funny	see	did	that	from	some
go	the	do	there	give	stop
help	three	eat	they	going	take
here	to	four	this	had	thank
I	two	get	too	has	them
in	up	good	under	her	then
is	we	have	want	him	think
it	where	he	was	his	walk
jump	yellow	into	well	how	were
little	you	like	went	just	when
		must	what	know	
		new	white		
		no	who		
		now	will		
		on	with		
		our	yes		

Let's Put It Together

Sometimes we take two words and join them together to make one word. We call these words *compound words*. Sound out these words. Sound out the first part of the word while covering up the second part. Then sound out the second part of the word. Put the two parts together. What word is it?

door mat	doormat
flash light	flashlight
rain storm	rainstorm
inch worm	inchworm
after noon	afternoon
moon light	moonlight

☺ Let's Make a Match

Draw a line to match the first part of each compound word with its second part.

hot   ball

beach   ship

space   dog

snow   light

flash   storm

🐭 How Quickly Can You Read?

These words are getting ready for a snowstorm! How quickly can you read the entire page? Ask your teacher to time you as you read the words. Cross out each word as you read it.

signal ribbon traffic jacket perfect

pocket cornmeal camel comet rocket

cactus within

batter boxcar puppet suntan

spaceship radish

I read this page in: _____

It's Time to Read!
Congratulations! You've learned so much about reading that you're ready to start reading your first real book! It's time to read Chapter 1 in *God's Big Story* Level 1.

Sound Recognition

Look at these letters. When they come at the end of a word, they say *ul*. Can you sound out these words?

le

little	**cattle**	**bottle**
tattle	**kettle**	**battle**
rattle	**turtle**	

Here are two more words with our new ending. In these words, the T is silent; it doesn't make any sound.

castle   **whistle**

Try these words, too. In the first word, the A will make an *uh* sound. In the second word, the I is a long vowel, so it will say its name.

apostle   **people**

Bible

Let's Make a Match

Read the sentences. Then circle the correct picture.

I will pick up the little bug.

The girl is reading the Bible.

The little boy has a bottle.

Billy likes to whistle.

 How Quickly Can You Read?

Look at all the words on this castle! Can you read them all? Cross out each word after you've read it correctly. Have your teacher time you as you read.

turtle　castle

battle　rattle

title

whittle

Bible　wring

whistle

wrap

wrestle

wrote　wrist

tattle

wreck　apostle

bottle
kettle

little

brittle

cattle

bustle　write

settle

I read this page in: _____

Activity Time!

It's time to complete the activities for Chapter 1 in
God's Big Story Level 1 workbook.

Lesson 93

Sound Recognition

Here's another sound to learn. These letters say *ong* as in *song*. Can you read these words?

ong

long	**wrong**
dong	**strong**
bong	**along**
song	

Here's a new word to learn. This word has two vowels in it, but both vowels are short.

devil

🐾 Fill in the Blank

Read the sentences. Choose the correct word to complete each sentence. Write the correct word in the blank. Then color the picture.

We walked for a _____ **time.**
bong strong long

Matt and Min drink and sing a _____ **.**
wrong song bong

The horse is big and _____ **.**
strong along dong

Let's Read a Story

This turtle is taking a trip somewhere. Where do you think he's going? Read his rhyming story to find out. This story uses a new word. This word is *today*.

today

Where Will I Go?

I am going away.
I will leave today.
I will walk a long, long way.
Where will I go?

I see the road is long.
But I am big and strong.
I will walk and sing a song.
Where will I go?

I am going to see Frog.
He sits down in the bog.
We will rest up on his log
For his birthday party!

 Optional Writing Practice

Choose one of the sentences from Turtle's story and write it beside the birthday frog.

Happy Birthday

It's Time to Read!

It's time to read Chapter 2 in *God's Big Story* Level 1.

🦒 Sound Recognition

Look at these letters. Do you remember what sound they make? We've learned that they say *ee* as in *bead*. But they also have another sound. They can say *e* as in *head*. This list of words uses our new *-e* sound. Sound out the words.

ea

head	**breath**
dead	**death**
bread	

Now sound out these words with our new e sound. Sound out the first part of the word, then add the second part.

fea ther	feather
Hea ther	Heather
hea ven	heaven
heavy	
health	

🐾 Fill in the Blank

Read the sentences. Choose the correct word to complete each sentence. Write the correct word in the blank. Then color the picture.

Min has a plate. The plate is not _____ .

dead   head   heavy

May I try a slice of your nice hot _____ ?

head   breath   bread

Heather found a _____ **from a red, blue, and yellow bird.**

heaven   feather   heather

Let's Read a Story

Today we have a special story to read. This is a story Jesus told. It's called a parable. A parable is a story that teaches a lesson. Sound out these words before you read the story. Remember to start by sounding out the first part of the word. Then sound out the last part of the word. Then put both parts together to see what they say.

king dom kingdom   **mus tard** mustard

com pare compare   **small est** smallest

A Tale about a Little Seed

What is the kingdom of heaven like? And to what shall I compare it? It is like a mustard seed. A man took the seed and put it in his garden. A mustard seed is the smallest of all seeds. But when it is grown, it is bigger than the plants. It grows into a tree, so the birds of the air can come and nest in it.

Great job! You're reading the Bible! Do you have a Bible of your own? You can find this parable in Matthew 13:31-32 and in Luke 13:18-19.

Optional Writing Practice

Read the sentences and copy them onto the lines below.

The kingdom of heaven

_____

- -

_____

Would you eat bread?

_____

- -

_____

My head is heavy.

_____

- -

_____

Activity Time!

It's time to complete the activities for Chapter 2 in
God's Big Story Level 1 workbook.

Be careful! These words are tricky!

Sound Recognition

Today we're going to learn some words that don't follow the rules. Most of these words have a silent E at the end, but the first vowel in each word makes a short vowel sound. Can you sound out these words?

give	river
live	have
forgive	promise

Sometimes a vowel makes the wrong sound. In these words, the O makes an *uh* sound, just like a U.

love	shove
dove	above
glove	

And sometimes O makes an *oo* sound.

move	prove

Let's Read a Story

Here is a strange creature. Read what the creature is saying. Do you know what kind of animal he is?

What Can I Be?

I am not yellow. I am not black. I do not have ten legs. I live under the sea. I love to swim all day. When I move, I swish in the sea. I shove the shells out of my way. I love the sea! Can you tell what I am?

Read the words on the octopus' sign. Can you find these words in the story you just read? If you can find them, circle the words on the sign. Cross out any words that are not in the story.

love

above

live

move

have

🦏 How Quickly Can You Read?

These words have decided to take a swim with the octopus. How quickly do you think you can read them? Have your teacher time you as you read. Can you read the words faster a second time? Try it and see!

long	devil	feather	live	glove
dong	today	Heather	forgive	shove
bong	head	heaven	river	above
song	dead	heavy	have	move
wrong	bread	health	promise	prove
strong	breath	kingdom	love	
along	death	give	dove	

I read this page in: _____

🐮 Sound Recognition

Today we have a new sound to learn. When a word ends in *-ind*, sometimes the I makes a long I sound and says its name. Can you read these words?

ind

find	**bind**	**grind**
kind	**rind**	
mind	**blind**	
be hind	behind	
un wind	unwind	
re mind	remind	
un kind	unkind	

Let's Read a Story

Do you like to read scary stories? Matt might get scared in this story. What do you think he sees? In this story, he takes a trip to the swamp. This story has two new words. Here they are:

swamp　　　　　　　　scary

Matt at the Swamp

Matt said, "I am going to the swamp. I hope I can find some thing to see. What kind of bugs live in a swamp? Will I find a beetle?"

Matt is looking for a beetle. Look out behind you, Matt! What is that scary thing?

Matt said, "I see a big thing with sharp teeth. It has green scales. Is it nice? Is it kind? Or is it mean? Is it unkind?"

What is this big green thing? Can you tell what it is? Matt is afraid of it.

Look out, Matt! This thing might eat you! Run, Matt, run!

Matt will run fast. He got away! Poor Matt had a scary day.

How Quickly Can You Read?

This alligator isn't happy. He wants to chomp all these words, but he doesn't know how to read. Can you read the words so he can eat them? How quickly do you think you can read them all? Have your teacher time you as you read. Write down how long it took you. Can you read them faster a second time? Try it and see!

Heather   breath   bread

obey   they   world

head

death   dead   away

unwind   enjoy   bind   worth

behind

grind   kind   destroy   worm

attack

blind   mind

find

heavy   feather   worse

heaven

afraid   adore

apart   alike   worst

word   about

amount   advice   agree   awake

allow   across   aware

I read this page in: _____

It's Time to Read!

It's time to read Chapter 3 in *God's Big Story* Level 1.

Sound Recognition

When we read, we see dots and marks at the end of sentences. Do you remember what these marks are called? They are called *punctuation marks*. Each mark has a special name.

. **period**

? **question mark**

! **exclamation point**

These marks come at the end of a sentence. Usually, a sentence ends with a period. If the sentence is making a statement or telling about something that happened, it probably ends with a period. But if the sentence is asking a question, it will end with a question mark. If something very exciting or scary happens in the sentence, it might end with an exclamation point.

Fill in the Blank

Read the sentences. Then add the correct punctuation to the end of each sentence.

Will you please find the turtle_____

The donkey ate its food_____

Look out for that shark_____

We packed a picnic lunch_____

Did Matt clean up his room_____

My First Bible Verses

Here's a new Bible verse for you to read. Ask your teacher if you need help sounding out the blue words.

You shall love the Lord your God with all your heart, with all your soul, and with all your mind.
Matthew 22:37

How Quickly Can You Read?

These words are stuck in the swamp. Can you read them before they get lost in the mud? How quickly do you think you can read them all? Ask your teacher to time you as you read. Write down how long it took you to read the words. Can you read them faster a second time? Try it and see!

would   played   work   worth   worm   lasted

allow   bread   away   Heather

couldn't   breath   closed   jumped

worst

looked   about   ended

dead   talked

shouldn't

head   amount

across

loaded   feather   from

awake   world   yelled   adore   heavy

should   wouldn't   could   word

I read this page in: _____

Activity Time!

It's time to complete the activities for Chapter 3 in *God's Big Story* Level 1 workbook.

Let's Put It Together

Do you remember the sounds that the letter C can make? Sometimes it says *ck* as in *can*, and sometimes it says *ss* as in *cent*. If an E or an I come after the letter C, the C will make a *ss* sound. Can you sound out these words?

cell

cent

city

circle

circus

citrus

These words have long vowel sounds. Try to sound them out.

cedar

cease

🐯 Fill in the Blank

Read the sentences. Choose the correct word to complete each sentence and write the word in the blank.

I saw a big tiger at the _____.

cedar   circus   citrus

This is a penny, and it is worth one _____.

cell   cease   cent

How many houses are in the _____?

city   citrus   cedar

How Quickly Can You Read?

These circus animals are ready to play. But all these words have gotten in their way. How quickly do you think you can read them all? Ask your teacher to time you as you read. Write down how long it took you to read the words. Can you read them faster a second time? Try it and see!

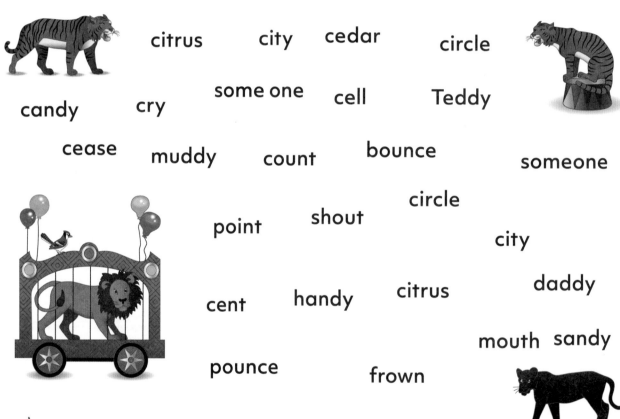

citrus　　city　　cedar　　　circle

candy　　cry　　some one　　cell　　Teddy

cease　　muddy　　count　　bounce　　　someone

circle

point　　shout

city

cent　　handy　　citrus　　daddy

mouth　sandy

pounce　　　　frown

I read this page in: _____

It's Time to Read!

It's time to read Chapter 4 in *God's Big Story* Level 1.

Sound Recognition

Look at these letters. We've seen them before. Sometimes they make the sound *ear* as in *hear*. But sometimes they make a different sound. In the words below, they make the sound *er* as in *earth*.

ear

earth   heard

earn   search

learn   yearn

Let's Make a Match

Read the sentences. Draw a line to match each sentence with the correct picture.

The sun is bigger than the earth.

Can a duck learn to read?

I heard the rooster crow.

What is the rabbit searching for?

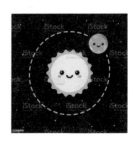

 Let's Read a Story

Read the story.

The Singing Catfish

Teddy said, "I am searching for a catfish. I think I heard one singing. I have to find this catfish." Teddy ran to Mom. He said, "Mom, where do you think I will find one? If I look in the bathtub, will it be there?"

Mom said, "No, it is not in the bathtub."

"Catfish must like to hide," Teddy said. "Do you think it is hiding in the trashcan? I will look and see." He looked in the trashcan, but there was not one there.

Teddy shook his head. "No, it isn't in the trashcan. Should I look in the attic? No, it can't be in the attic. I must learn how to search the house. Where could the catfish be?"

Teddy found Dad in the yard. "I am searching for a catfish," Teddy told Dad. "Where could it be? Will you give me a clue?"

Dad gave a smile. "Yes, I will give you a clue," he said. "Could the catfish be outside the house?"

"Yes," said Teddy. "I will search outside. Should I look in the lake? Yes, let's look in the lake!"

Teddy raced to the lake. What did he see? He saw a big catfish. The catfish was singing. He sang, "Come eat with me! I cook in the sea!"

"You are a silly catfish," Teddy said. "You are singing and cooking in the lake!"

🐘 Optional Writing Practice

Read the words and copy them onto the lines below.

A catfish was singing.

‾‾‾‾‾‾‾‾‾‾‾‾‾‾‾‾‾‾‾‾‾‾‾‾‾‾‾‾‾‾‾‾‾‾‾‾‾‾
- -
_____

Will you search for a fish?

‾‾‾‾‾‾‾‾‾‾‾‾‾‾‾‾‾‾‾‾‾‾‾‾‾‾‾‾‾‾‾‾‾‾‾‾‾‾
- -
_____

Dad will help you find it.

‾‾‾‾‾‾‾‾‾‾‾‾‾‾‾‾‾‾‾‾‾‾‾‾‾‾‾‾‾‾‾‾‾‾‾‾‾‾
- -
_____

Activity Time!

It's time to complete the activities for Chapter 4 in
God's Big Story Level 1 workbook.

Lesson 100

Sound Recognition

Sometimes words don't sound the way we think they should. Look at this word. Listen as your teacher sounds it out. Then read the word by yourself.

Je sus   Jesus

When two vowels come together in a word, the first vowel is long and says its name. Sometimes the letter Y pretends to be a vowel too. In these words, the first vowel is long because of the letter Y. The Y is making an E sound in these words.

baby   **lady**   **shady**

🦝 Fill in the Blank

Read the sentences. Choose the correct word to complete each sentence. Write the word in the blank.

A _____ place is a nice place to sit.

baby   lady   shady

A _____ can be loud when it is crying.

baby   lady   shady

Will that _____ wash the floor?

baby   lady   shady

⬤ How Quickly Can You Read?

Frog has decided to hop home to his house. But look at all these words surrounding his house! How quickly do you think you can read them all? Have your teacher time you as you read. Then write down how long it took you to read all the words. Can you read them faster a second time? Try it and see!

river

learn

yearn   heard   bind   find   love   dove

search   obey   blind   bread

give   creature

forgive   breath   glove

feather

heaven   kind   they   vulture

mind   unwind

live   pasture

wind

rind   Scripture

death   above   behind

have

I read this page in: _____

It's Time to Read!

It's time to read Chapter 5 in *God's Big Story* Level 1.

🐵 Let's Put It Together

Look at this toy train. Whose do you think it is? Read the sentence to find out.

This train is Lily's.

We know the train belongs to Lily because the sentence tells us. See the S at the end of Lily? That S and the little mark beside it tell us that Lily owns the train. The little mark is called an *apostrophe*. When we want to show that someone owns something, we add an apostrophe and an S to the end of their name.

🐾 Fill in the Blank

Read the sentences. Choose the correct word to complete each sentence. Write the word in the blank. Remember that we need to add an apostrophe and an S to show who owns something.

This toy truck is _____ .

Billy's   Billy   Billys

That is _____ **turtle.**

Billy's   Billy   Billys

I would like to ride on _____ **tractor.**

Billy's   Billy   Billys

_____ **box is big and tall.**

Matts   Matt's   Matt'

🐀 How Quickly Can You Read?

Look at the big box Matt has! Do you think he could fit all these words inside the box? Read the words as quickly as you can. Then color Matt and his box.

rattle   settle   cattle   from

kettle   wrist   come

bustle

turtle   apostle

tattle   wrestle

along

little   strong   why

wreck

wrong   castle   title

bong

wring   whistle

dong

Bible

song   long   wrath   wrap

sword   write

wrote

 I read this page in: _____

🦒 Sound Recognition

Here are some new words to learn. You've read one of them before. Listen as your teacher reads these words. Then try to read them yourself. They don't follow the rules we've learned, so you must remember what they sound like whenever you see them.

camel   **water**   **woman**

🐻 Let's Put It Together

Sometimes two words join together to make one big word. Sound out these words.

him self   himself

her self   herself

some one   someone

some times   sometimes

be fore   before

bedtime

sunshine

snowball

Let's Draw a Picture

Read the sentences. Then draw a picture to show what each sentence is about.

Sometimes it will snow.

Someone ate the pie.

I am ready for bedtime.

Optional Writing Practice

Read the words and copy them onto the lines below.

Billy's dump truck

_____
- -
_____

A loud teakettle

_____
- -
_____

Look out for the snowball!

_____
- -
_____
- - - - - - - - - - - - - - - - -
_____

It's Time to Read!

It's time to read Chapter 6 in *God's Big Story* Level 1.

● Let's Put It Together

Look at this word. What does it say? If we have one dog, we write it like this.

dog

But if we have more than one dog, we add an S to the end of the word to show that there are more than one. We call this the *plural form*.

dogs

Sometimes we add *-es* to the end of a word to show that there are more than one. Read these words.

pig	**pigs**
pot	**pots**
plate	**plates**
dish	**dishes**
box	**boxes**

🐾 How Many?

Read the words. If the word says there is only one of something, color that word green. If the word says there is more than one, color that word red.

ships   foxes
picnic   pickle
beaches   hotdogs
hands   tree

How Quickly Can You Read?

How quickly do you think you can read these words? Have your teacher time you as you read. Can you read the words faster a second time? Try it and see!

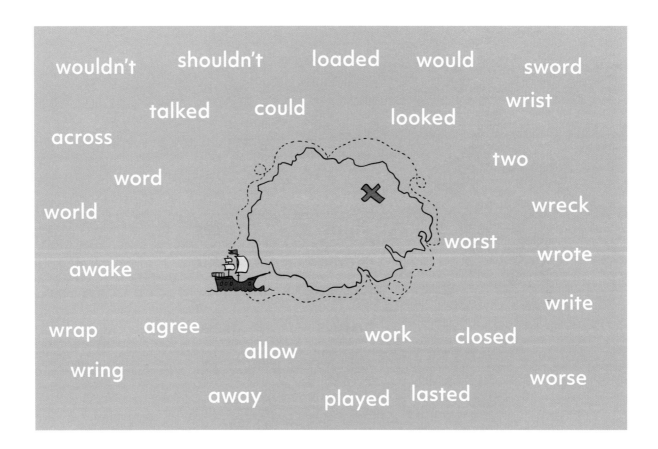

wouldn't   shouldn't   loaded   would   sword

talked   could   looked   wrist

across   two

word   wreck

world   worst   wrote

awake   write

wrap   agree   work   closed

allow

wring   worse

away   played   lasted

I read this page in: _____

Activity Time!

It's time to complete the activities for Chapter 6 in *God's Big Story* Level 1 workbook.

🦒 Sound Recognition

These words all end with the same sound. Try to sound them out by yourself. If you need help, ask your teacher to sound out the first one for you.

tired

hired

fired

mired

wired

expired

retired

Here's another word to learn. Try to sound it out by yourself. If you need help, ask your teacher.

mercy

🐱 Fill in the Blank

Read the sentences. Then add the correct punctuation to the end of each sentence.

The baby got tired after lunch_____

Did God have mercy on Abraham____

Dad hired a new person to help with the work____

Do you have ten boxes left____

Find the Right Word

Look at the picture. Choose a word from the box that describes the picture. Write the word on the line. Then color the picture.

mired	expired	hired	retired
wired	tired	fired	

_____

- -

_____

How Quickly Can You Read?

How quickly do you think you can read these words? Have your teacher time you as you read. Can you read the words faster a second time? Try it and see!

camp	creature	they	sprint
feature	Scripture	water	spring
capture	milk	help	obey
bump	silk	nature	pasture
cask	strap	future	wrap
mask	sprang	gulp	
self	sulk		
golf	bulk		
strip	bask		
scrub	damp		
gulf	dump		
string			

 I read this page in: _____

It's Time to Read!

It's time to read Chapter 7 in *God's Big Story* Level 1.

Sound Recognition

Today we have a new sound to learn. When a word ends in -ull, sometimes it says *ull* like in *gull*, and sometimes it says *ull* like in *pull*. Can you read these words?

ull

gull

lull

skull

pull

full

bull

🦝 Fill in the Blank

Read the sentences. Choose the correct word to complete each sentence. Write the word in the blank.

Will you please _____ **on the rope?**

gull   pull   bull

I fed a cracker to the _____ .

gull   lull   full

That _____ **has large horns.**

gull   pull   bull

🦁 Let's Draw a Picture

Read the sentence. Then draw a picture to show what is happening in the sentence.

The seagull landed on the brown bull.

My First Bible Verses

Here is a new Bible verse. You can read all the words in this verse!

The earth, O Lord, is full of Your mercy.
Psalm 119:64

Optional Writing Practice

Read the sentences. Then copy them onto the lines below.

My skull is hard.

_____
- - - - - - - - - - - - - - - - - -
_____

The wind pulls the kite.

_____
- - - - - - - - - - - - - - - - - -
_____

Is the glass full yet?

_____
- - - - - - - - - - - - - - - - - -
_____

🦒 Sound Recognition

Look at these words. Sometimes our letter O makes a different sound. In these words, it makes the sound *uh* like in *other*. Sound out these words.

other

mother

brother

smother

another

Here's another word with an O that makes an uh sound:

color

🐯 Let's Make a Match

Read the sentences. Draw a line to match each sentence with the correct picture.

My brother is eating his birthday cake.

This is another toy train set.

What color is that small lizard?

Ask Mother before you paint with that brush!

🦏 How Quickly Can You Read?

How quickly do you think you can read these words? Have your teacher time you as you read. Can you read the words faster a second time? Try it and see!

another   brother   color   give   live

other   water   dove

smother   frown   come   howl

crow   mother   have   from   glove   bowl

grow   above

growl   river   owl

lull   gull   cow   skull

pull   full   low   snow

pow   blow   enjoy

love   bull   destroy

I read this page in: _____

Activity Time!
It's time to complete the activities for Chapter 7 in
God's Big Story Level 1 workbook.

Sound Recognition

Here's a new sound. When these two letters come together in a word, they say *f* as in *phone*. Sound out these words. Ask your teacher if you need help.

ph

phone

pho nics   phonics

Jo seph   Joseph

pro phet   prophet

graph

Philip

Ralph

🐼 Fill in the Blank

Read the sentences. Fill in the blank with the correct word to complete each sentence.

I will call you on my _____ .

photo　phone　phonics

_____ help me learn to read.

phone　graph　phonics

Please give these grapes to _____ .

graph　Philip　phone

Let's Make a Match

Read the sentences. Circle the sentence that matches the picture. Then color the picture.

My mother is looking at her phone.

My dad is looking at his phone.

It's Time to Read!

It's time to read Chapter 8 in *God's Big Story* Level 1.

Sound Recognition

Today we have a new sound to learn. When a word ends in -ild, sometimes the I makes a long I sound and says its name. Can you read these words?

ild

wild   **mild**   **child**

Sometimes vowels come together and make a strange sound. Look at this ending. These letters say *ild* as in *build*.

uild

build   **guild**   **rebuild**

Find the Right Word

Look at the pictures. Choose a word from the box and write it below the correct image.

| guild   mild   wild   build   child |

_____   _____   _____
- - - - - - - - - -   - - - - - - - - - -   - - - - - - - - - -
_____   _____   _____

🦁 Let's Read a Story

This story has two new words in it. Ask your teacher to sound out the words for you. Then try to read them by yourself in the story.

Egypt   **Herod**

A Little Child and a Bad King

When Jesus was a little baby, King Herod tried to kill Him. King Herod sent men to find Jesus and kill Him. But God told Joseph to run away and hide so the bad men could not kill Jesus. Joseph and Mary took their child to another land. They took Him to a land called Egypt. King Herod could not kill Jesus in this land. Jesus stayed in Egypt until King Herod died. Then His mother and Joseph took Jesus back to their home. God kept baby Jesus safe from a bad king.

You can read the rest of this history in the Bible. It's found in chapter two of the book of Matthew.

🐾 How Quickly Can You Read?

These children are going on a trip to Egypt, and all these words have decided to come along. How quickly do you think you can read these words? Have your teacher time you as you read. Can you read the words faster a second time? Try it and see!

I read this page in: _____

Activity Time!

It's time to complete the activities for Chapter 8 in *God's Big Story* Level 1 workbook.

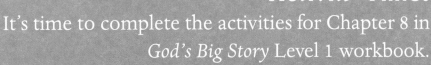

🦛 Sight Words

Here are some new words to learn. These words don't follow the rules we've learned. Listen as your teacher reads them. Then read them by yourself. Can you remember what each word says? You'll need to memorize these words.

here   **want**

four   **once**

pretty   **again**

busy

Here are some more words that don't sound the way we think they should. Try sounding them out. If you need help, ask your teacher.

prison

risen

slither

famine

children

Fill in the Blank

Read the sentences. Choose the correct word to complete each sentence and write the word in the blank.

The judge will send the

bad man to _____ .

risen   prison   pretty

That is a _____ bird.

here   prison   pretty

I have three grapes, but you have

_____ of them.

again   four   once

 How Quickly Can You Read?

Here is a list of sight words you've learned already. How quickly do you think you can read them all? Have your teacher time you as you read.

and	two	have	want
away	where	four	obey
come	famine	pretty	could
down	you	busy	water
here	all	out	forgive
once	are	she	live
look	again	soon	walk
my	good	there	were
said	from	they	when

 I read this page in: _____

It's Time to Read!

It's time to read Chapter 9 in *God's Big Story* Level 1.

🐷 Let's Put It Together

Look at these two letters. Do you remember what sounds they make? They can make three different sounds. What are they? Look at the chart and sound out the words.

ed

ed as ed	ed as d	ed as t
ended	yelled	picked
lasted	closed	walked
handed	filled	talked
landed	played	camped

Fill in the Blank

The door is locked.

Now you get to make your own chart! Sound out each word in the box. What sound does its ending make? Write the word in the column with the correct ending.

lasted	killed	locked	hooked	camped
loaded	fitted	talked	spotted	willed
walked	played	ended	closed	filled

ed as ed	ed as d	ed as t

🦏 How Quickly Can You Read?

How quickly do you think you can read these words? Have your teacher time you as you read. Can you read the words faster a second time? Try it and see!

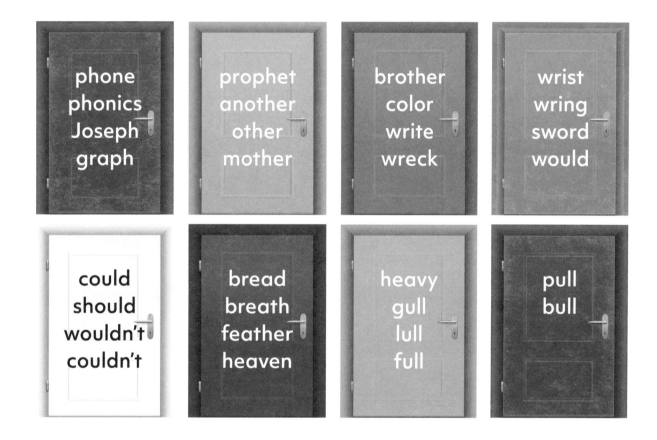

phone phonics Joseph graph	prophet another other mother	brother color write wreck	wrist wring sword would
could should wouldn't couldn't	bread breath feather heaven	heavy gull lull full	pull bull

I read this page in: _____

Activity Time!

It's time to complete the activities for Chapter 9 in *God's Big Story* Level 1 workbook.

🐒 Let's Put It Together

Look at this sentence. See the first letter of the sentence? It is a capital letter. Whenever we write a sentence, we make the first letter big. We capitalize the letter.

We went to the zoo.

If there is a name in the sentence, we capitalize the name too. We also capitalize words that talk about God.

Pam and Teddy went to the zoo.

🐹 Fix the Sentence

In these sentences, someone forgot to capitalize the first letters. They forgot to capitalize the names too. Can you fix this mess? If a letter is supposed to be capitalized, cross out the letter. Then write the capital letter above it.

god made the earth and all things.

did matt and min find a bug?

i will give a letter to sally.

we should thank god for our food.

How Quickly Can You Read?

Do you remember Teddy's singing catfish in Lesson 99? The catfish finished making his supper, and he has invited all these words to come eat with him. How quickly do you think you can read them all? Ask your teacher to time you as you read. Write down how quickly you read the words. Can you read them faster a second time? Try it and see!

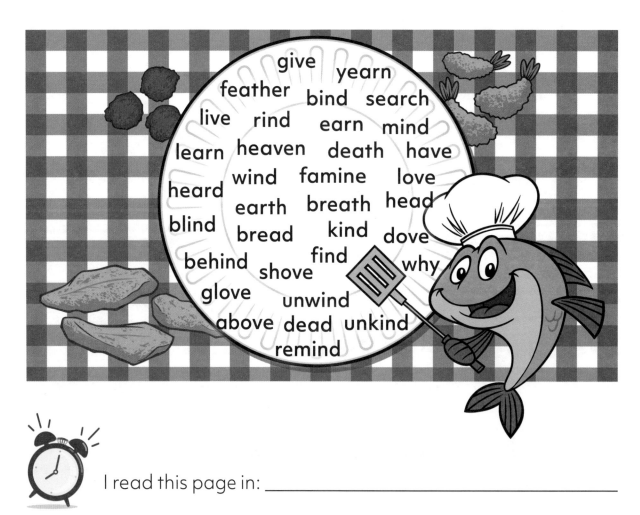

give
yearn
feather bind search
live rind earn mind
learn heaven death have
wind famine love
heard
earth breath head
blind
bread kind dove
behind find why
shove
glove
unwind
above dead unkind
remind

I read this page in: _____

It's Time to Read!

It's time to read Chapter 10 in *God's Big Story* Level 1.

Sound Recognition

Here's a new sound to learn. When K and N come at the beginning of a word, the K is silent and doesn't make any sound. Sound out these words with a silent K.

kn

knit	**knelt**	**knuckle**
knitting	**knock**	
knee	**knight**	

Here are some more words with a silent K. The *-ow* in these words makes the *O* sound as in *know*.

know	**known**	**knowing**

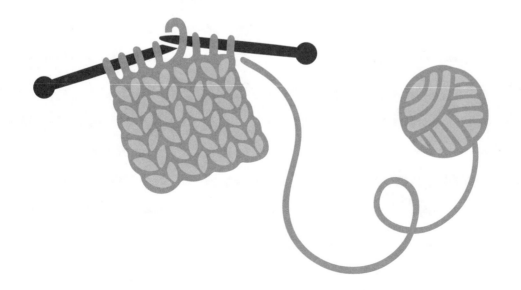

🐻 Let's Make a Match

Read the sentences. Find the sentence that matches the picture. Draw a line from that sentence to the picture.

The knight knelt in front of the king.

The knuckle knelt in front of the throne.

The knight knelt in front of the queen.

🐉 How Quickly Can You Read?

Look at all the words surrounding this dragon. How quickly do you think you can read these words? Have your teacher time you as you read. Can you read the words faster a second time? Try it and see!

knelt　　　knight　　kick

knitting　　walk

knock

phonics　knee　　work

known　graph　　knit

prophet　　phone

knuckle

kindle

Philip

Ralph

knowing　know

I read this page in: _____

Activity Time!

It's time to complete the activities for Chapter 10 in *God's Big Story* Level 1 workbook.

Sound Recognition

Here's a new sound to learn. The -ew in these words says *ew* as in *new*. Sound out the words.

ew

dew

new

blew

stew

chew

These words are spelled the same as the ones you just read, but they make a different sound. Listen as your teacher reads them. Then read them by yourself.

few

pew

🐾 Fill in the Blank

Read the sentences. Choose the correct word to complete each sentence. Write the word in the blank.

We sit in a _____ **at church.**

few   pew   chew

It is good to _____ **your food before you swallow it.**

few   new   chew

The tall knight has a _____ **sword.**

new   stew   dew

Let's Put It Together

Whenever we write a sentence, we make the first letter big. We capitalize the letter. If there is a name in the sentence, we capitalize the name too. Here are two new names to learn.

Israel

Israel ite   Israelite

An Israelite is a person from Israel.

Capitalize the names in the following sentences.

matt rode a camel from israel. He went to see egypt.

It's Time to Read!
It's time to read Chapter 11 in *God's Big Story* Level 1.

Sound Recognition

Here are some new words to learn. In these words, the letter A makes a new sound. It makes an *ah* sound like in *father*. Sound out these words with our new sound.

mama   **papa**   **father**

● Let's Make a Match

Read the sentences. Find the sentence that matches the picture. Draw a line from that sentence to the picture.

Mama found the ball on the beach.

My brother and I found the ball on the beach.

My father is taller than my mother.

My mother is taller than my father.

🐀 How Quickly Can You Read?

This mouse has decided to take a trip to the beach. These words want to come along with him. How quickly do you think you can read them all? Ask your teacher to time you as you read. Write down how long it took you to read the words.

papa

mama

knelt

stew

chew   knight

know

new

knit

blew   grew

knock

dew

knee

crew

few   flew

knowing   water

knitting

father

threw

pew

known

knuckle   nephew

I read this page in: _____

Activity Time!

It's time to complete the activities for Chapter 11 in *God's Big Story* Level 1 workbook.

Lesson 115

 ## Sound Recognition

Look at these words. You've seen some of them before. Sometimes words change when we make them plural. *Plural* means we're talking about more than one thing. If we have more than one puppy, we say *puppies*. If we have more than one penny, we say *pennies*. Sound out these words and their plural forms. Notice how the letter Y disappears when the word becomes plural.

puppy	puppies
penny	pennies
copy	copies
city	cities
sky	skies
try	tries
baby	babies

🐻 Let's Put It Together

All these words end in the letter Y. If we want to say that there is more than one of something, we take off the Y and add -ies. Look at the words below. Make each of these words plural by taking off the Y and adding -ies. Then color the picture.

baby   babies

sky   skies

bunny   _____

spy   _____

candy   _____

body   _____

🦝 Fill in the Blank

Read the sentences. Choose the correct word to complete each sentence. Write the word in the blank.

Will you knit with the _____ ?

copies   pennies   ladies

Father said I can _____ to ride the bike.

tries   try   babies

How will the frog catch the _____ ?

spies   flies   cities

🦏 How Quickly Can You Read?

All these words are confusing the frogs so they can't catch their dinner. Can you help by reading the words? How quickly do you think you can read them all? Ask your teacher to time you as you read. Write down how long it took you to read the words.

cry   try   tries   skies   spies   candies

spy   bunnies   shady   cries   flies   babies

lady   where   pennies   cities   copies

there

ladies   puppies   busy   here   four   sky

risen

want   once   again   prison

pretty

I read this page in: _____

🦒 Sound Recognition

Do you remember what sound the letter G makes if it comes before an E? It makes a soft G sound, as in *gem*.

gem

If G comes before an I, it will make the same soft sound. Try reading these words.

gem   **age**   **bridge**

germ   **cage**

gin

giant

en gine   engine

lo gic   logic

gi raffe giraffe

🦝 Fill in the Blank

Read the sentences. Choose a word from Giraffe's signs to complete each sentence.

giant
cage
bridge
engine
gentle

I keep my pet mice in a

_____ .

Did your car _____ stop working?

In the Bible, David will fight a big _____ .

I will be _____ when I pet the cat.

Trains cross on that _____ .

● Let's Put It Together

Here are two more words with a soft G sound. These words both start with the letter A. The A makes a long vowel sound in these words.

angel

agent

As you read, remember that G will usually have a soft sound if it comes before E or I.

It's Time to Read!

It's time to read Chapter 12 in *God's Big Story* Level 1.

 Sound Recognition

Today we have a new sound to learn. This is a sound the letter U makes. Listen as your teacher reads these words. Then try reading them by yourself.

put

push

bush

 Sight Words

Here are some new words to learn. These words don't follow the rules we've learned. Listen as your teacher sounds them out. Then read them by yourself. Can you remember what each word says? You'll need to memorize them.

many

any

young

Let's Make a Match

Read the sentences. Draw a line to match each sentence with the correct picture.

Jane will trim the bush.

Min is pushing the baby.

Please help wash the dishes and put them away.

How many books do you have?

● How Quickly Can You Read?

Here are some tricky words to read. Be careful as you sound them out! How quickly do you think you can read them? Have your teacher time you as you read. You will probably read the words faster a second time. Try it and see!

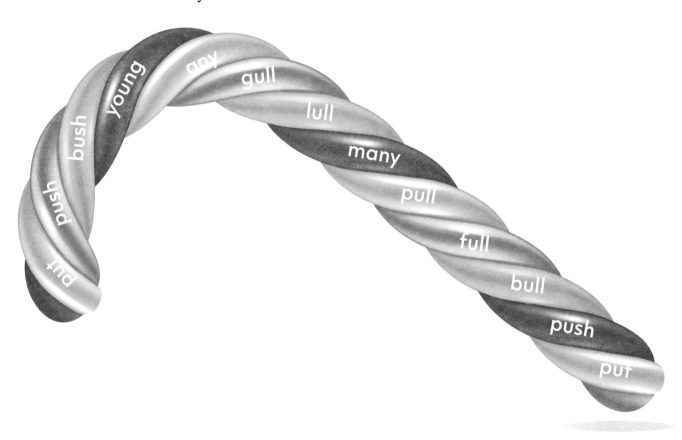

 I read this page in: _____

Activity Time!
It's time to complete the activities for Chapter 12 in *God's Big Story* Level 1 workbook.

✿ Let's Put It Together

Do you remember what an apostrophe is? It's a little mark that goes above the letters in a word. Sometimes this mark is used to show us who owns something. An S and an apostrophe at the end of a word show us that someone owns something.

Bob's car

🐆 Find the Right Word

Read the phrases below. If the words tell us who owns something, circle the words. If the words don't tell us who owns something, cross them out.

Jill's dress   Joseph's dream

Two pennies   Grass hills

Jack's coat   Giant cats

Bunnies hop

Sight Word Review

Do you remember how these words sound? Read them silently to yourself. Then read them out loud as quickly as you can. Ask your teacher to mark any word you get wrong. Can you read the words correctly the next time? Try it and see!

stage   page   dodge   agent

gem   cage

once   water

age   angel

bridge   young   put   bush

giant   push

engine

logic   earn

giraffe   any

young   many

earth

It's Time to Read!

It's time to read Chapter 13 in *God's Big Story* Level 1.

🌑 Let's Put It Together

We've learned a lot about vowels. We've learned short vowel sounds and long vowel sounds. Now it's time to learn some rules about the long vowel sounds. You already know most of these rules.

Rule 1

If two vowels are beside each other in a word, the first vowel says its name, and the second vowel is silent. If a word ends in an E, the E will be silent, and the other vowel in the word will be long.

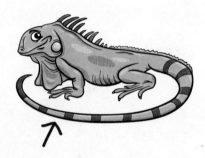

tail　　　**meet**　　　**cake**　　　**bake**

Rule 2

If a word ends with a vowel and that vowel is the only vowel in the word, the vowel will make a long vowel sound.

we　　　　**he**　　　　**go**　　　　**no**

Some words don't follow our two rules. Here are some words that don't follow the rules. You've learned some of these already. If you need help sounding out the others, ask your teacher.

do   **done**   **money**

to   **none**   **honey**

If a word has two vowels, sometimes both vowels make short vowel sounds.

desert   **lemon**   **lizard**

A snake in the desert

😊 Let's Make a Match

Read the sentences. Find the sentence that matches the picture. Draw a line from that sentence to the picture.

I would not like some honey.
He is eating the honey.

Are you done baking yet?
Are you done cleaning yet?

Please put the money in the wig.
Please put the money in the pig.

The turtle has a shell, but the lizard has none.

The turtle has a shell, but the lemon has none.

Activity Time!

It's time to complete the activities for Chapter 13 in *God's Big Story* Level 1 workbook.

🐞 Sound Recognition

Look at these letters. We learned about them in Lesson 75. These letters say *ou* as in *out*. Sound out these words.

ou

shout	**found**
mouse	**ground**
couch	**sound**

Sometimes these letters make a different sound. If these letters join together with -ght, they make a sound like *-ought* as in *thought*. Sound out these words.

ought

fought   **thought**   **ought**   **bought**

Sometimes this sound is spelled with an A instead of an O.

aught

taught   **caught**   **daughter**

Fill in the Blank

Read the sentences. Choose the correct word to complete each sentence. Write the word in the blank.

My father has three _____ .

caught   ought   daughters

My mother _____ me how to read.

sought   taught   brought

We _____ the shopping bags home with us.

ought   brought   caught

🐻 How Quickly Can You Read?

Here are some tricky words to read. Be careful as you sound them out! How quickly do you think you can read them? Have your teacher time you as you read. You will probably read the words faster a second time. Try it and see!

brought   caught   slaughter   money

sought   daughter   live

bought   taught

                                                   forgive   honey

ought   any

                                          desert   young

thought

                                                   push   bush

fought

sound

ground   put   many

found   angel

agent   germ

house

I read this page in: _____

Sound Recognition

Here's a new sound to learn. We've seen this sound before. Usually it says *-ear* as in *fear* or *-ear* as in *earth*. But sometimes it says *-air* as in *bear*. Sound out these words with our new sound.

ear

bear   **tear**

pear   **wear**

Good job! Here are some more words that use these same sounds.

break   **steak**

🐻 Let's Put It Together

Read the sentences. Then choose one of the sentences and draw a picture to show what the sentence is about.

"Mother, may I wear this raincoat?"

The bear is eating all the pears.

Father is cooking a steak.

Let's take a break and rest a little.

🦏 How Quickly Can You Read?

Look at that scary bear! Do you think he'll eat all these words? Try to read them all before he does. How quickly do you think you can read them? Have your teacher time you as you read. Can you read the words faster a second time? Try it and see!

break   steak   dodge   engine

bear   agent   gem   cage   giraffe

angel   why   push

age   stage   put   bush

tear   bridge

wear

young

pear   many   young

young   giant   any

logic

Matt sees a bear.

I read this page in: _____

Activity Time!

It's time to complete the activities for Chapter 14 in *God's Big Story* Level 1 workbook.

Sound Recognition

Here are some letters we've seen before. These letters say *pro* as in *prophet*. Sound out the words.

pro

profit   **prosper**

project   **problem**

proverb

Sometimes the O in these letters will make a long vowel sound. In some words, these letters say *pro* as in *protect*. Sound out these words with a long O sound.

protect   **proceed**

profess   **prolong**

provide

Whenever you see -pro, you'll need to sound out the rest of the word to know whether the O is making a long or short sound.

Reading Comprehension

Read the questions and find the correct answer. Write *yes* or *no* in the blank.

Will God protect His people? _____

Do you know all the problems in math? _____

Can you find the book of Proverbs in the Bible? _____

Will a mother bear provide food for her young bear cubs? _____

😺 Let's Put It Together

Just like in the words *provide* or *protect*, sometimes the first vowel in a word will make a long vowel sound, and the second vowel will make a short vowel sound. Look at these words. The first vowel is long, and the second vowel is short. Can you sound out the words?

refill   relax   respect   reprint   resist

🦝 Fill in the Blank

Read the sentences. Choose the correct word to complete each sentence and write the word in the blank.

I like to go outside and _____ in the sun.

respect   reprint   relax

God wants us to _____ dad and mom.

refill   respect   resist

It's Time to Read!

It's time to read Chapter 15 in *God's Big Story* Level 1.

Sound Recognition

Remember that sometimes the letter T is silent in a word. It won't make any sound at all. Sound out these words. Pretend that the T isn't there.

listen

glisten

fasten

hustle

bustle

🐿 Finish the Sentence

Read the sentences. Then add a period or a question mark at the end of each sentence. Remember that you should use a question mark if the sentence is asking a question.

Did you listen to what Father said_____

Please help me fasten this button_____

I hear a rustle in the grass outside_____

Do your brothers like to wrestle_____

📖 My First Bible Verses

Here is a new Bible verse. In this verse, the Lord talks to Samuel, and Samuel responds. Can you read the verse by yourself?

Now the Lord came and stood and called as at other times, "Samuel! Samuel!" And Samuel said, "Speak, for Your servant listens."
1 Samuel 3:10

How Quickly Can You Read?

Mama bear and her cubs are playing with words. Can you read these words to the bears? How quickly do you think you can read them? Have your teacher time you as you read. Can you read the words faster a second time? Try it and see!

listen
glisten
fasten
hustle
bustle
rustle
wrestle

relax
refill
respect
refund
resist
reprint
respond

proper
profit
project
proverb
problem
promise
prophet

protect
profess
provide
proceed
learn
heard

I read this page in: _____

Activity Time!

It's time to complete the activities for Chapter 15 in *God's Big Story* Level 1 workbook.

🦒 Sound Recognition

Here are two letters we've seen before. These letters often appear at the beginning of a word. They are called a *prefix*. A prefix is something that comes at the beginning of a word. Sound out these words with the prefix *be*. The E in this prefix makes a long vowel sound.

be

began

begin

begun

below

being

behold

belong

behind

beloved

🐻 Let's Put It Together

Read the sentences. Then choose one of the sentences and draw a picture to show what the sentence is about.

On Day Five, the sharks were made.

The bird said, "This fish belongs to me."

The frog is hiding behind the mushroom.

David became the king of Israel.

🦒 Let's Make a Rhyme

Read the words. Circle the words that rhyme with *fare*.

care

bear

dark

pear

near

water

dare

far

where

How Quickly Can You Read?

Bear and his friends have come to help you read. How quickly do you think you can read these words? Have your teacher time you as you read. Can you read the words faster a second time? Try it and see!

know	knuckle	stew	dew
knit	known	chew	threw
knee	knowing	new	nephew
knight	father	grew	few
knelt	water	blew	pew
knock	mama	crew	
knitting	papa	flew	

I read this page in: _____

It's Time to Read!

It's time to read Chapter 16 in *God's Big Story* Level 1.

🐮 Sound Recognition

We've learned that when two vowels come together, the first one says its name, and the second one is silent. But sometimes vowels don't obey this rule. Sometimes they do things backwards. Isn't that silly? Here are some words with vowels doing things backwards. In these words, the first vowel is silent, and the second vowel is a long vowel sound.

thief   **priest**

chief   **belief**

field   **believe**

shield

👧 My First Bible Verses

Here is a new Bible verse. Try to read this by yourself. If you need help, ask your teacher to help you sound out the word in bold.

Believe on the Lord Jesus Christ, and you will be saved.

Acts 16:31

Let's Read a Story

Here's a story to read. There are three new words in this story. Two are little words, and one is a big word. Listen as your teacher reads the little words. Then read the big word by yourself. Try to sound it out a little at a time.

who   else

sal-a-man-der   salamander

Who Will You Invite?

Matt and Min are having a tea party.

"We will have the tea party in a field," Min said. "I will serve a piece of cake."

"Who should we invite to the party?" Matt asked.

"We should invite the baby bears," Min said.

"Who else?" Matt asked.

"Let's invite Sammy the salamander," said Min.

"That's a good plan!" Matt said. "Now I want to invite someone."

"Who will you invite?" Min asked.

"I will invite Dickie." Matt said.

"Please do not invite Dickie," Min said. "Dickie is a thief. He will steal my piece of cake."

"Dickie is a thief," Matt said. "But I will tell him not to steal your piece of cake."

Who is Dickie? Do you know? We must wait and see.

🐭 How Quickly Can You Read?

These words have decided to come to Matt and Min's tea party. How quickly do you think you can read these words? Have your teacher time you as you read. Can you read the words faster a second time? Try it and see! Then color the picture.

behold   belong   behind   beloved   behave   beware   betray

being

below   become   beyond

begun   before   beneath

begin   because

who   besides

believe

belief   else   chief   pierce   field   grief

shield   priest   fierce   yield   niece

I read this page in: _____

🐄 Sound Recognition

Look at these letters. When these letters come together, they make the sound *-erry* as in *cherry*. Sound out these words.

erry

cherry   **merry**

berry   **ferry**

Sometimes the letters *-arry* make the same sound as the letters above. Sound out these words.

arry

marry

carry

tarry

🐾 Finish the Sentence

Read the story. Add a period or a question mark at the end of each sentence. Remember that you should use a question mark if the sentence is asking a question.

Matt will carry a plate_____

What is on the plate_____

Matt has a piece of cherry pie on his plate_____

What will Matt do with the cherry pie_____

He will carry it to the dragon_____

What is the dragon's name_____

The dragon's name is Dickie_____

🦏 How Quickly Can You Read?

Oh, dear! Dickie's cousin has decided to burn up all these words. Can you read them before he sets them on fire? How quickly do you think you can read them all? Have your teacher time you as you read. Can you read the words faster a second time? Try it and see!

cherry	carry	
berry	tarry	
niece	hustle	
shield	below	
chief	being	
begin	relax	
begun	refill	
belief	their	
believe	come	bustle
pierce	grief	wrestle
fierce	field	respect
began	priest	earth
fasten	listen	earn

I read this page in: _____

Activity Time!

It's time to complete the activities for Chapter 16 in *God's Big Story* Level 1 workbook.

🦒 Sound Recognition

We've read these words before. Do you remember how to sound them out?

night

sight	**right**
night	**fright**

Here are some words that are similar to the ones you've already learned. Each of these words has three of the same letters in it. These letters say *igh* as in *high*. Try to sound out these words. Some of the words are tricky. If you need help, ask your teacher to help you.

My head is up high!

igh

high

sigh

thigh

🐻 Let's Put It Together

Look at these words. Find the *igh* in each word. Color these letters red. Then sound out the words. Some of these words are tricky. If you need help, ask your teacher to help you.

right	**higher**	**mighty**
sigh	**tonight**	**alright**

🐾 Fill in the Blank

Read the sentences. Choose the correct word to complete each sentence. Write the word in the blank.

A bat flies at _____ .

fight   night   slight

Is the boy's kite _____ than the girl's?

mighty   flight   higher

Will you come to my party _____ ?

tonight   sigh   fight

● How Quickly Can You Read?

How quickly do you think you can read these words? Have your teacher time you as you read. Can you read the words faster a second time? Try it and see!

fight	slow	alright	honey
light	sigh	fought	desert
their	high	thought	pull
tonight	higher	bought	full
slate	delight	their	bull
low	mighty	money	

I read this page in: _____

It's Time to Read!
It's time to read Chapter 17 in *God's Big Story* Level 1.

🦒 Sound Recognition

You've learned some of these words before. Try to read every word on this list. Circle any words that are difficult for you to read.

one	three	five	seven	nine
two	four	six	eight	ten

1 2 3 4 5 6 7 8 9 10

The number *eight* is a strange word to read. We've seen part of this word in other words. Do you remember how to sound out these words?

sigh   **night**   **right**

When the letters *-igh* come together, they say *-igh* as in *high*. But if these letters have an *-e* with them, they will say *-eigh* as in *weigh*. Sound out these words with our new *-eigh* sound.

weigh   **eight**   **neigh**

sleigh   **weight**

Find the Match

Read the sentences. Then draw a line to match each sentence with the correct picture.

They are riding in a red sleigh.

How much do I weigh?

I will listen to the horse neigh.

The little bat is flying at night.

🐾 Let's Put It Together

Sometimes we add some extra letters to the end of a word to make it a new word. Sound out these words. Then add the ending letters to make a new word. Sound out the new word.

 four + th = fourth

 seven + th = seventh

eight + th = eighth

Try writing these new words. Then sound them out.

ten + th = _____

six + th = _____

Great job!

Activity Time!
It's time to complete the activities for Chapter 17 in *God's Big Story* Level 1 workbook.

🦛 Let's Review

Here are some sight words you've seen before. These words don't follow the rules we've learned. Do you remember how each of these words sound? Read the words.

here	pretty	want	again
four	busy	once	who

🦛 Sight Words

Here are some new words to learn. Listen as your teacher reads the words. Then read them by yourself.

every

among

does

friend

holy

Will you be my friend?

Finish the Sentence

Read the sentences. Then add a period, question mark, or exclamation point at the end of each sentence. Remember that you should use a question mark if the sentence is asking a question. If something very exciting or scary happens in the sentence, you should use an exclamation point.

. **period**

? **question mark**

! **exclamation point**

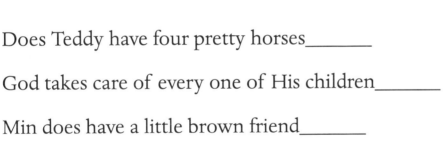

Does Teddy have four pretty horses_____

God takes care of every one of His children_____

Min does have a little brown friend_____

Look out for that snake_____

My First Bible Verses

Here's a new Bible verse for you to read.

A friend loves at all times.

Proverbs 17:17

How Quickly Can You Read?

How quickly do you think you can read these words? Have your teacher time you as you read. Can you read the words faster a second time? Try it and see!

here	city	among
four	again	does
pretty	water	holy
want	who	friend
seventh	every	eight
once	ever	shout
busy	else	believe

I read this page in: _____

It's Time to Read!

It's time to read Chapter 18 in *God's Big Story* Level 1.

Sound Recognition

Here's a new sound to learn. This sound says *-tion* as in *nation*.
Sound out these words.

tion

nation	**action**
station	**fiction**
lotion	**portion**
motion	

Great job! Now try to sound out these words. Sound them out one
piece at a time. Then put the pieces together and sound out the
whole word.

a-dop-tion	adoption
do-na-tion	donation
e-lec-tion	election

🐹 Fill in the Blank

Read the sentences. Choose the correct word to complete each sentence. Write the word on the line.

May we please go see the train _____ ?

nation   lotion   station

If a story is not true, we say it is _____.

portion   fiction   motion

If a dad and mom adopt a child,

this is called _____ .

donation   election   adoption

🐻 Let's Make a Match

Read the sentences. Find the sentence that matches the picture. Draw a line from that sentence to the picture.

When I go to the beach, I put on some lotion.

When I go to the beach, I put on some motion.

Sally is working on fictions.

Sally is working on fractions.

 How Quickly Can You Read?

Dickie the Dragon wants to see how quickly you can read these words. How quickly do you think you can read them? Have your teacher time you as you read. Can you read the words faster a second time? Try it and see!

action	donation	does
station	bear	once
lotion	wear	who
motion	tear	every
portion	they	ever
fiction	obey	never
election	busy	their
adoption	here	want
fraction	again	friend
section	pretty	holy
nation	among	

 I read this page in: _____

Activity Time!

It's time to complete the activities for Chapter 18 in *God's Big Story* Level 1 workbook.

🦒 Sound Recognition

In our last lesson, we learned that the letters *tion* say *-tion* as in *nation*. Look at these four letters. They also say *-sion*, like in *mission*. Sound out these words.

sion

passion

session

vision

version

mission

tension

in-va-sion   invasion

 **Let's Read**

Read the sentences.

Look out! Here comes an ant invasion!

These glasses will help your vision.

 **Sorting It Out**

Read these words. If a word ends in *tion*, write the word in the first box. If the word ends in *sion*, write the word in the second box.

motion	vision	nation	invasion	station
action	version	mission	lotion	passion

tion	sion

How Quickly Can You Read?

These ants need to get from one anthill to the other. Can you help them by reading a path of words for them to follow? How quickly do you think you can read these words? Have your teacher time you as you read. Can you read the words faster a second time? Try it and see!

action   session   pear   wear

tear

they

obey

never   pretty   four   here   destroy   enjoy

knee

knowing   among   does   once   busy

their

who

every

promise

prophet

want   friend   holy

I read this page in: _____

It's Time to Read!

It's time to read Chapter 19 in *God's Big Story* Level 1.

Sound Recognition

Here are some words you've seen before. Some of these words don't follow the rules we've learned. Do you remember how each of these words sound? Read the words.

many	**slither**	**river**
any	**prison**	**famine**
young	**risen**	**children**

🐱 Finish the Sentence

Read the sentences. Then add a period or a question mark at the end of each sentence. If a letter needs to be capitalized, cross the letter out and write the capital letter above it.

it's time to eat some dinner_____

my friend, ted the turkey, is a good cook_____

ted the turkey baked a pie_____

do you like to eat cherry pie_____

🐻 Let's Read

Read the sentences silently to yourself. Then read them out loud as quickly as you can. Color the picture.

A chicken is on a mission.

A toad is in the snow.

A sleigh got in the way.

A shield is in the field.

How Quickly Can You Read?

These snakes want to hear you read. How quickly do you think you can read these words? Have your teacher time you as you read. Can you read the words faster a second time? Try it and see!

any

many

young

slither

why

risen

large

giraffe

prison　ridge　　river　　giant

gorge

engine　mama

logic

father　famine　lady

papa

candies

tries

shady

children

I read this page in: _____

Activity Time!

It's time to complete the activities for Chapter 19 in *God's Big Story* Level 1 workbook.

Sound Recognition

Here's a new sound to learn. These letters say *sure* as in *measure*. Do you see the -ea in some of these words? This -ea makes a short -e sound.

sure

sure

measure

treasure

pleasure

pressure

leisure

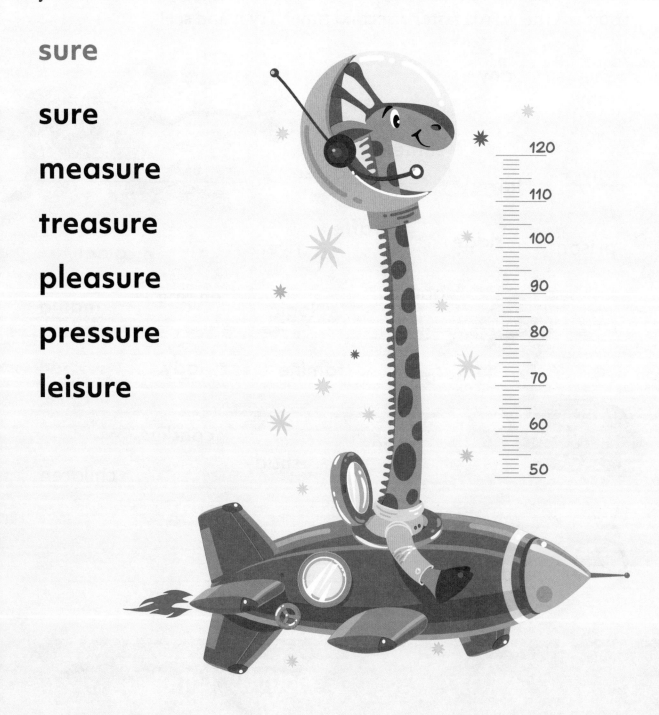

120

110

100

90

80

70

60

50

🐱 Fill in the Blank

Read the sentences. Choose a word from the box to complete each sentence.

pleasure	measure	treasure	sure

Let's _____ to see how tall you are.

Are you _____ this is the right way to go?

Matt and Min found some _____ .

It is a _____ to meet you.

My First Bible Verses

Here's a new Bible verse for you to read.

I rejoice at Your word like someone who finds great treasure.
Psalm 119:162

Let's Make a Match

Read the sentences. Circle the sentence that matches the picture. Then color the picture.

It is a measure to eat ice cream.

It is a pleasure to eat ice cream.

It's Time to Read!
It's time to read Chapter 20 in *God's Big Story* Level 1.

Sound Recognition

In our last lesson, we learned the *-sure* sound. Now we'll learn another sound that is almost the same. This sound says *-ture* as in *capture*. Can you sound out these words?

ture

capture

picture

fracture

Scripture

Let's Make a Match

Look at the pictures. Choose a word from the box and write the word under the correct picture.

capture	picture	treasure	measure

_____

- -

_____

_____

- -

_____

_____

- -

_____

_____

- -

_____

🦓 Find the Sound!

Read the pairs of words. If the pair of words rhymes, color the words. If the words don't rhyme, cross them out.

nation   measure

station   treasure

mission   capture

pleasure   action

🐀 How Quickly Can You Read?

How quickly do you think you can read these words? Have your teacher time you as you read. Can you read the words faster a second time? Try it and see!

capture	sure	version	water
Scripture	leisure	learn	donation
picture	invasion	heard	section
fracture	vision	action	station
measure	session	election	portion
treasure	mission	nation	fiction
pleasure	passion	lotion	adoption

 I read this page in: _____

Activity Time!

It's time to complete the activities for Chapter 20 in *God's Big Story* Level 1 workbook.

🐶 Sound Recognition

In Lesson 115, we learned about the plural forms of words. Do you remember what this means? *Plural* means a word is talking about more than one thing. If we have one dog, we say *dog*. But if we have more than one dog, we add an S to the end of the word and say *dogs*.

Sometimes words change how they are spelled when we make them plural. Look at these words. All these words end in *-ife*. When we make these words plural, the F will change to a V. Read the words.

wife	wives
life	lives
knife	knives

Some words that end in -f or -fe act the same way. Look at these words. Read the words and the sentence.

safe	saves
leaf	leaves
loaf	loaves

Our God is a God who saves.

🐵 Let's Put It Together

Look at these words. Some of them end in -ife, and some of them end in the letter Y. If we want to make the word plural and say that there is more than one of something, we will need to change the end of the word. Do you remember how to do this? The first few words are done for you. If you need more help, look back at Lesson 115.

baby   babies

sky   skies

wife   wives

puppy   _____

knife   _____

copy   _____

try   _____

loaf   _____

🐱 How Many?

Read the words. If a word is in the plural form, color the word blue.
If the word is not plural, color the word red.

puppies

leaves

nation

beaches

picture

wives

lives

copies

treasure

action

How Quickly Can You Read?

How quickly do you think you can read these words? Have your teacher time you as you read. Can you read the words faster a second time? Try it and see!

here	pretty	among	allow
four	want	talked	played
busy	once	across	work
again	two	never	worse
does	sword	ever	lasted
friend	would	word	away
wrap	could	awake	closed
write	shouldn't	wring	
wrote	wouldn't	wrath	
wrist	who	loaded	
holy	every	agree	

I read this page in: _____

Sound Recognition

You've learned that the letters -ch make a -*ch* sound as in *chocolate*. But sometimes these letters make a -*ck* sound instead. Read these words. In these words, -ch will make a -*ck* sound.

chord   **school**

chorus   **scheme**

Christmas   **scholar**

Christ

Now try to sound out these two words.

character   **Christian**

Christian is a tricky word. Look at the word closely so you'll remember how to pronounce it next time you see it. Here are two other words that make a similar sound. Can you sound these out? If you need help, ask your teacher.

musician   **special**

🐯 Let's Make a Match

Read the sentences. Circle the sentence that matches the picture.
Then color the picture.

I will finish my school work.

This is what we do at Christmas.

The musician is playing.

🐭 Let's Put It Together

Read the sentences. If -ch is making a *-ck* sound, color it red. If -ch is making a *-ch* sound, color it purple. Then color the picture.

I go to church on Sunday.

Mommy said we can play after we finish school.

Sometimes it is cold and chilly at Christmas.

Min will choose the pretty shell.

 How Quickly Can You Read?

How quickly do you think you can read these words? Have your teacher time you as you read. Be careful! These words are tricky! Can you read them faster a second time? Try it and see!

chorus

chopping

school

such

teacher

scholar

chill

much

chicken

scheme

Christ   chord   Christmas

checked

character

earn

chin   beach

Christian

earth

I read this page in: _____

It's Time to Read!

It's time to read Chapter 21 in *God's Big Story* Level 1.

🦒 Sound Recognition

Do you remember the two sounds that the letter G makes? Sometimes it makes a hard sound and says *g* as in *goat*. But sometimes it makes a soft sound and says *j* as in *gem*. Sound out these words. Be careful of the G!

gem	age	stage	grin	huge
germ	cage	ridge	bridge	
get	logic	giraffe	engine	
giant	game	goat	judge	

That last word sounds a little strange. The U makes the same sound that it does in *mule*. We heard this sound in *musician* in our last lesson. Now sound out these new words. The U in these words makes the same sound as in *huge*.

use	cue	confuse
fuse	cute	puny
music	cube	musician

Let's Put It Together

Read the sentences. If G is making a hard sound (like in *goat*), color it brown. If G is making a soft sound (like in *cage*), color it green. Remember that G will usually have a soft sound if it comes before an E or an I.

The giraffe is much taller than the little goat.

Does the judge wear a badge like the police man?

Give this green Christmas card to Sally, and give the huge card to Phil.

Matt tried to cross the bridge, but his engine stopped working.

🦝 Fill in the Blank

Read the sentences. Choose the correct word to complete each sentence. Write the word on the line.

May I have two ice _____ **please?**

cubs   cubes   tubes

Jenny said she likes to listen to the _____ **.**

midge   mustard   music

If something is big, we may say it is _____ **.**

hugs   huge   germ

How Quickly Can You Read?

How quickly do you think you can read these words? Have your teacher time you as you read. Can you read the words faster a second time? Try it and see!

mustard

cute

cut   cube

music

confuse   pickle

monkey   puny

use

cue   pencil

kitten

accuse

huddle

fuse   amuse

chorus   hungry

treasure   footprint

musician   excuse   huge

Christian   special

picture

I read this page in: _____

Activity Time!

It's time to complete the activities for Chapter 21 in *God's Big Story* Level 1 workbook.

🦒 Sound Recognition

You've learned the sound that the letter H makes. But sometimes the letter H is silent and won't make any sound at all. Look at these words. In these words, H doesn't say a thing. Sound out the words, but don't sound out the letter H. If you need help, ask your teacher.

hour   **herb**

honor   **heir**

honest   **ghost**

honestly

🐕 Read It and Draw

Read the words. Then draw a picture to match the words.

Look at this cute puppy!	Daddy is coming in one hour.	I show honor to old people.

🐻 Let's Make a Match

Read the sentences. Circle the picture that matches the sentences.

Do you see that little boy? He is not being honest. He is stealing a cookie.

📖 My First Bible Verses

Here's a new Bible verse for you to read.

Honor your father and your mother, that your days may be long upon the land which the Lord your God is giving you.
Exodus 20:12

How Quickly Can You Read?

These animals want you to read to them. How quickly do you think you can read these words? Have your teacher time you as you read. Can you read the words faster a second time? Try it and see!

help	use	honestly	motion	cube
hour	fuse	music	fracture	pull
how	pleasure	cute	confuse	bull
hold	leisure	witness	heir	push
honor	honest	fraction	ghost	put

 I read this page in: _____

It's Time to Read!

It's time to read Chapter 22 in *God's Big Story* Level 1.

🍎 Let's Put It Together

Do you remember learning about capitalization? We always capitalize the first letter of a sentence. If there is a name in the sentence, we capitalize the name too. We also capitalize words that talk about God. Read these sentences.

Daddy took Billy and me to the store.

We will praise and worship God.

We also capitalize the days of the week and the months of the year. Can you read these words?

Sunday	January
Monday	February
Tuesday	March
Wednesday	April
Thursday	May
Friday	June
Saturday	July
	August
	September
	October
	November
	December

🦝 Fill in the Blank

Read the sentences. Write the correct word in the blank to complete each sentence. If you need help with spelling, look at the lists of days and months above. Don't forget to capitalize the names of the days and months!

Today is _____ .

My birthday is in the month of _____ .

We go to church on _____ .

Christmas comes in _____ .

Remember to capitalize names, days, and months

🦝 Fix the Sentence

In these sentences, someone forgot to capitalize all the letters that need to be capitalized. Can you fix this mess? If a letter is supposed to be capitalized, cross it out. Then write the capital letter above it.

god gave us a special day for rest.

this day is sunday.

should we do school on thursday?

i will read with pam and matt on friday.

will it rain or snow in december?

bob's birthday is in june.

 How Quickly Can You Read?

How quickly do you think you can read these words? Have your teacher time you as you read. Can you read the words faster a second time? Try it and see!

March	Sunday	November	water
Thursday	honor	December	confuse
hour	October	heir	Wednesday
May	honest	Tuesday	September
January	Saturday	February	July
	cube	Monday	confusing
	honestly	cute	August
	April	knock	
	Friday	knight	

 I read this page in: _____

Activity Time!

It's time to complete the activities for Chapter 22 in
God's Big Story Level 1 workbook.

🐻 Find the Opposite

All words have a meaning. Some words mean the same thing as other words. But some words mean the opposite of other words. Look at these two words. Do they mean the same thing, or do they mean the opposite?

hot   cold

If two words mean opposite things, we call those words *antonyms*. Read these words. Draw a line to match each word to its opposite. If you need help sounding out the first word, ask your teacher to help you.

quiet	old
hot	long
young	loud
little	big
weak	cold
short	strong

☺ Find the Same Meaning

Some words have the same or almost the same meaning as other words. We call these words *synonyms*. Read these words. Draw a line to match each word to a word that has the same or almost the same meaning.

fast	wealthy
small	giant
rich	hard
huge	quick
difficult	little

☺ Let's Make a Match

Read the words. Then draw a picture to match the words.

It rained on Wednesday.	We go to church in the morning.	This giraffe is huge!

🐭 How Quickly Can You Read?

Look at these two pictures of Min. These pictures show opposite things. As you read the words on this page, look for a word that shows what Min is doing in each picture. Circle the words. After you've finished reading all the words on the page, color the pictures.

vision	bread	Heather	heavy	behind
version	awake	feather	find	unwind
mission	passion	heaven	mind	remind
head	session	tension	bind	
healthy	breath	invasion	blind	
wealthy	death	asleep	grind	

I read this page in: _____

🐵 Let's Put It Together

Do you remember the alphabet? Can you say it by yourself? Sometimes we use the alphabet to put things in order. When we do this, we call it *alphabetizing*. Let's alphabetize some words. If a word starts with A, that word will be at the top of our list. If a word begins with Z, it will be last, at the end of the list. Read this list of words.

apple

dog

fish

goat

jump

kite

pickle

snake

vase

zoo

● Putting Things in Order

Read these words. Then put them in alphabetical order. If a word begins with A, put that word at the beginning of the list. Then look for a word that starts with B. Next comes a word that starts with C. Use the alphabet to help you put the words in the correct order.

ax _____

wagon _____

dish _____

boat _____

hand _____

cat _____

egg _____

🐾 Fill in the Blank

Read the sentences. Choose the correct word to complete each sentence. Write the word on the line. Remember to check for capital letters!

On _____ , we had a picnic in the garden.
friday   Friday   furry

It is good to _____ our father and mother.
honest   owned   honor

Min has a music lesson on _____ .
thirsty   thursday   Thursday

How Quickly Can You Read?

How quickly do you think you can read these words? Have your teacher time you as you read. Can you read the words faster a second time? Try it and see!

count	eight	hound	skate
bounce	sleigh	found	enjoy
pounce	giraffe	weigh	destroy
bear	frown	neigh	shout
pear	round	howl	trout
down	tear	growl	break
clown	wear	weight	steak

I read this page in: _____

It's Time to Read!

It's time to read Chapter 23 in *God's Big Story* Level 1.

Sound Recognition

We've learned that the letters -ie often make a long E sound. Read these words. See how the I comes before the E in every word?

Watch the ei and ie!

chief　　**field**　　**priest**　　**belief**　　**believe**

Sometimes these letters will switch around, and the E will come before the I. This happens when they come after a C. They still usually make a long E sound.

receive　　　　**deceit**　　　　**conceit**

ceiling　　　　**deceive**　　　　**conceive**

But sometimes -ei will make an A sound. You've already learned these words. Do you remember how to sound them out?

weigh　　　**weight**

sleigh　　　**neigh**

eight

I before
E except
after C
Or when it
says A
As in
reindeer
or neigh.

This -ie and -ei sound is a little tricky, so we have a jingle to help us remember how it works. Can you memorize this?

🦝 Fill in the Blank

Let's make a chart with our -ie and -ei words. Sound out these words and put them in the correct column.

Field	receive	yield	sleigh	deceit
Ceiling	pierce	reindeer	chief	weigh
Neigh	conceive	believe	conceit	eight

ie as ee	ei as ee	ei as ay

How Quickly Can You Read?

Look at the words falling with the snow! How quickly do you think you can read them all? Have your teacher time you as you read. Can you read the words faster a second time? Try it and see!

again who here holy four pretty
every bustle listen wrestle
beloved friend rustle
never fasten
want does
among respect
once
glisten behold resist
relax
began below

refund being
begin
reprint

I read this page in: _____

Activity Time!

It's time to complete the activities for Chapter 23 in *God's Big Story* Level 1 workbook.

🐞 Let's Put It Together

We have many words in our language. Each word tells us something. Some words tell us the name of a thing. We call these words nouns. A *noun* is a word that tells us the name of a person, place, or thing. Read this list of nouns.

dog **flower** **Friday** **Mommy**

Kate **book** **church**

🐯 Find the Nouns

Read the words beside this picture. If a word is a noun, circle it. If a word isn't a noun, cross it out.

bear **rock** **hat**

kitten **spider** **were**

going **was** **Sally**

🐢 Here Comes the Action!

Some words tell us the name of a person, place, or thing. These words are *nouns*. Other words tell us what a person or thing is doing. These are action words that show us what is happening. An action word is called a *verb*. Read this list of verbs. Can you act out what is happening?

running   **flying**

walk   **eating**

jumped   **slept**

raining

🐢 Fill in the Blank

Someone took all the verbs out of these sentences. There are no words to tell us what is happening. Can you fix these sentences? Choose a verb from the box and write it in the blank. Remember that a verb should show you what is happening. A verb will show action.

jumped	snowed	fox	swimming
yellow	rained	crying	swam
ran	yelling	below	fierce

I _____ to the store.

Baby Jill is _____ again.

The grass is wet because it _____ outside.

We will go _____ at the pool today.

 How Quickly Can You Read?

How quickly do you think you can read these words? Have your teacher time you as you read. After you've read the words once, color all the nouns red. Then color all the verbs green. Can you read the words faster a second time? Try it and see! Then color the pictures.

Peter	chewing
spacesuit	played
jumped	Bible
raining	cake
bedroom	baked
talking	kitten
chalk	barking
notebook	fishing
eat	battle
school	praying

I read this page in: _____

It's Time to Read!

It's time to read Chapter 24 in *God's Big Story* Level 1.

Let's Put It Together

Do you remember what a verb is? It is a word that shows action. Sometimes it shows action that has already happened, like in this sentence:

I walked to the door.

Sometimes it shows action that is happening right now. Read this sentence:

I am walking to the door.

Sometimes a verb will tell us an action that is going to happen in the future. Read this sentence:

After I eat lunch, I will walk to the door.

If a verb tells us something that has already happened, we say it is a past tense verb. This means it is telling us something that already happened in the past.

If a verb tells us something that is happening right now, we say it is a present tense verb. This means it is telling us what is going on right now.

If a verb tells us something that hasn't happened yet, we say it is a future tense verb. This means it is telling us something that will happen later on in the future.

Find the Past Tense

Read the sentences. If a verb is telling us something that already happened in the past, circle the verb. Then write *past* on the line to show that this verb already happened.

I slept last night.

_____

I will finish school this afternoon.

_____

The cat ate his food yesterday.

_____

Five giraffes ran to the pond for water.

_____

I slept Saul will die in the battle.

_____

Putting Things in Order

Read these names. Then put them in alphabetical order. If a word begins with A, put that word at the beginning of the list. Then look for a word that starts with B. Next, look for a word that starts with C. Use the alphabet to help you put the words in the correct order.

Samuel _____

David _____

Hannah _____

Adam _____

Caleb _____

Moses _____

How Quickly Can You Read?

How quickly do you think you can read these words? Have your teacher time you as you read. Can you read the words faster a second time? Try it and see!

shady

some   from   lady   why

cactus   come   batter   our

              cornmeal

their   camel

                         puppet

        baby   prison   here

your

                              spaceship

        Jesus   rocket

were   wash   risen

within   water   again   pretty

          slither   want

suntan   four

        once

comet   children   famine

I read this page in: _____

Activity Time!

It's time to complete the activities for Chapter 24 in *God's Big Story* Level 1 workbook.

Let's Put It Together

Do you remember what a prefix is? A *prefix* is something that comes at the beginning of a word. A prefix will change a word's meaning. Read this word.

button

Now let's add a prefix. Here is the prefix -un. Add this to the word *button*. What new word do we have?

un + button = unbutton

Here are some more words with our prefix -un. Read these words and see how the prefix changes the meaning of the words. What do you think the prefix -un means?

happy	**unhappy**	
tie	**untie**	
glue	**unglue**	
unzip	**untidy**	**unsaved**
unwrap	**unholy**	**unwell**

🐾 Fill in the Blank

Look at the picture. Then read the sentences. Choose a word that matches the picture. Write the word on the line.

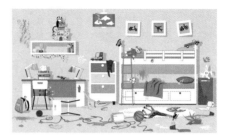

Bill's room is _____ .

tidy   untidy

The bed is _____ .

unmade   made

Bill should clean his room _____ .

Monday   Thursday   today

📖 My First Bible Verses

Here's a new Bible verse for you to read. In this verse, God is talking about His priests. In King David's day, priests were the ones who taught God's people what the Word of God said.

They shall teach My people the difference between the holy and the unholy.

Ezekiel 44:23

How Quickly Can You Read?

How quickly do you think you can read these words? Have your teacher time you as you read. Can you read the words faster a second time? Try it and see!

unripe   unwell   push
unhurt   eight
unroll
unwrap   unsafe
weight   unholy
untrue
neigh   weigh   agent
sleigh
angel   honestly
many   young
bush
cute   confuse   confusing

any
hour
put
use
honor
honest
music
cube

Do you like ripe or unripe bananas?

I read this page in: _____

It's Time to Read!

It's time to read Chapter 25 in *God's Big Story* Level 1.

🦒 Sound Recognition

Look at these words. You can sound them out easily, can't you?

race **place**

face **space**

Sometimes when -ace comes at the end of a word, it will make a different sound. Sometimes it will say *-iss*. Sound out these words, but when you get to the *-ace* at the end, pronounce it *-iss*.

palace **menace**

furnace **preface**

surface **grimace**

necklace

🦓 Let's Look at Syllables

All the words with our -iss sound have two parts to them. We call these parts *syllables*. We can break words into their syllables and sound them out a piece at a time. Sound out these words.

pal ace	palace
fur nace	furnace
neck lace	necklace
chick en	chicken

Sound out these syllables. Then put all the syllables together and write them on the line to make a word.

sur face _____

fam i ly _____

bas ket _____

cat er pil lar _____

How Many Syllables?

Some words have only one syllable. Other words have many syllables. One way to find out how many syllables are in a word is to clap. As you sound out a word, clap each time you pronounce a full sound. Watch as your teacher claps to count the number of syllables in these words.

duck   racetrack   pickle   family

Now you try it! Clap as you sound out these words. On the line, write how many syllables each word has.

picnic   _____

me   _____

monkey   _____

adoption   _____

forgive   _____

friend   _____

hippo   _____

September   _____

bedtime   _____

How Quickly Can You Read?

This knight is trying to get to the palace, but the words are in his way. Can you help by reading the words as quickly as you can? How quickly do you think you can read them? Have your teacher time you as you read. Can you read the words faster a second time? Try it and see!

palace   delight   alright   tonight   mighty   higher

necklace   scheme   leisure   pressure   measure

pleasure   fracture   treasure   earn   earth

Christmas   chord   character

Christ   palace

capture

Scripture

scholar   furnace

grimace

surface

Christian

surface

preface

necklace   special

menace   picture   furnace   school

I read this page in: _____

Activity Time!

It's time to complete the activities for Chapter 25 in *God's Big Story* Level 1 workbook.

🦒 Sound Recognition

Sometimes words don't sound the way we think they should. Look at these words and try to sound them out. If you need help, ask your teacher to give you a hint.

idea   only

idol   altar

iron

calf   animal

half   argue

aunt

tomato   message

potato   tomorrow

As you begin to read books, you'll find some words that you don't recognize. First, try sounding them out. If that doesn't work, ask someone for help. Remember that words are sometimes pronounced differently than we think they should be.

🐻 Let's Put It Together

Do you remember what a prefix is? A prefix is something that comes at the beginning of a word. A prefix will change a word's meaning. Here's a new prefix. Let's add this to a word and see what happens.

dis + obey = disobey

What do you think the prefix -dis means?

Here's another prefix. It means *to do something again*. Read this word.

re + tie = retie

🐱 Fill in the Blank

Read the sentences. Choose the correct word to complete each sentence. Circle the word.

I lost my picture, so I have to _____ it.
undraw   redraw   disdraw

Aunt Jane untied the _____ and gave it some grass.
half   calf   call

Did the puppy _____ you again?
disobey   unobey   reobey

How Quickly Can You Read?

There are some tricky words on this page. Matt is afraid you might not be able to read them all! Be careful as you sound them out. Remember that some words don't sound the way we think they should. How quickly do you think you can read them? Have your teacher time you as you read. Can you read the words faster a second time? Try it and see! When you're finished reading, color the pictures.

Can you read those hard words?

aunt   idea   idol   tomato   refill

only   half   calf   altar   iron

tomorrow   furnace   palace   surface   potato

argue   necklace   animal   message

measure   disobey   disagree   discover   rename

disown   disarm   distrust   menace   preface

resell   dislike   remind   rewrite   refresh   revisit

I read this page in: _____

It's Time to Read!

It's time to read Chapter 26 in *God's Big Story* Level 1.

🐄 Let's Put It Together

Do you remember what a verb is? It is a word that shows action. Sometimes it shows action that has already happened, and sometimes it shows action that is going to happen in the future. Read this sentence:

After I eat lunch, I will walk to the door.

If a verb tells us something that hasn't happened yet but is going to happen later, we say that it is a *future tense* verb. This means it is telling us something that will happen later on in the future. When a verb is a future tense verb, it will often have the word *will* before it.

Tomorrow I will milk the cow.

☺ Find the Past Tense

Read the sentences. If a verb is telling us something that will happen later on in the future, circle the verb. Underline the word *will* if it comes before the verb.

The pig read his book last night.

The raccoon will read later today.

Dolly washed the car and the truck.

We will go for a ride with Daddy on Monday.

I will learn my Bible verse tomorrow.

Putting Things in Order

Read these words. Then put them in alphabetical order. If a word begins with A, put that word at the beginning of the list. Then look for a word that starts with B. Next, look for a word that starts with C. Use the alphabet to help you put the words in the correct order.

idol

animal

mustard

palace

camel

octopus

🦏 How Quickly Can You Read?

These octopuses have decided to play dress-up. Do you know what they're pretending to be? After you finish your schoolwork, maybe you can play dress-up too! Read the words on this page. How quickly do you think you can read them all? Have your teacher time you as you read. Can you read the words faster a second time? Try it and see!

tomato	message	November
potato	aunt	December
only	palace	Tuesday
altar	March	February
idol	Thursday	Monday
iron	May	June
idea	January	Wednesday
calf	Sunday	September
half	October	July
animal	Saturday	August
tomorrow	April	
argue	Friday	

I read this page in: _____

Activity Time!

It's time to complete the activities for Chapter 26 in *God's Big Story* Level 1 workbook.

Sound Recognition

Sometimes the letter I makes a long E sound when it comes at the end of a word. But be careful! Sometimes it will also make a long E sound in the middle of a word. Sound out the words.

ski	chili	pizza
taxi	deli	safari
kiwi	zucchini	
mini	pepperoni	

🐾 Fill in the Blank

Read the sentences. Choose the correct word from the box and write it in the blank.

cow	taxi
pizza	head

Would you like pepperoni on your _____ ?

What kind of animal is Min milking? _____

Teddy has a blue hat on his _____ .

My family rode in a _____ when we went to the city.

Let's Draw a Picture

Read the sentences. Then draw a picture to show what is happening.

When I get hungry, I will eat lunch.

Daddy has eight animals to take care of.

🦏 How Quickly Can You Read?

These words have decided to go on safari! How quickly do you think you can read them? Have your teacher time you as you read. Can you read the words faster a second time? Try it and see!

kiwi	knowing	idea	potato	half
ski	knot	idol	animal	aunt
taxi	only	iron	message	palace
mini	altar	feather	tomorrow	
pizza	bread	heaven	argue	
zucchini	breath	heavy	calf	
safari	death	tomato		

 I read this page in: _____

It's Time to Read!

It's time to read Chapter 27 in *God's Big Story* Level 1.

🐄 A Look at Old English

Long ago, people used different words when they spoke English. Here are some words that people used to use every day. Have you heard these words before?

thee   **thou**

You may have heard these words when someone read the Bible to you. These words are the same as our word *you*. They mean the same thing. Today, we speak a little differently than people did long ago. If you want to ask someone how they're doing, which sentence would you use?

How are you?   **How art thou?**

Both these sentences mean the same thing, but the words are a little different.

🦁 Let's Read Old English

Read these sentences in Old English. Draw a line from each sentence to the sentence that says the same thing in modern English. Circle the Old English words that are different than the English words you speak today.

Thou hast both books.

Are you dry under the umbrella?

I will give thee a banana.

You have both books.

Art thou dry under the umbrella?

I will give you a banana.

Let's Read a Story

Here are some pieces of stories for you to read. You've probably heard these stories before. Can you guess what they are? One is found in Genesis chapter 3, and the other is in Luke 15. If you can't figure out what the story is, look it up in the Bible.

And the Lord God said unto the serpent, "Because thou hast done this, thou art cursed above all cattle, and above every beast of the field. Upon thy belly shalt thou go, and dust shalt thou eat all the days of thy life."

And the son said, "I will arise and go to my father, and will say unto him, 'Father, I have sinned against heaven, and before thee, and am no more worthy to be called thy son. Make me as one of thy hired servants.'" And he arose and came to his father. But when he was yet a great way off, his father saw him and had compassion.

After you finish reading, circle all the Old English words that we don't use today. Can you guess what these words mean?

Mine and Thine

One of the words you read in the stories above is the word *thy*. This word means *your*. In Old English, the words *you* and *your* looked very different. They looked more like our words *me* and *my*. Look at these words. Can you guess what the words in the second column mean?

me	**thee**
my	**thy**
mine	**thine**

**This is my ice cream,
and that ice cream is thine.**

🦒 Antonyms and Synonyms

Do you remember learning about antonyms and synonyms? If two words mean opposite things, we call those words *antonyms*. If two words mean the same or almost the same thing, we call them *synonyms*.

Antonym means opposite   **hot**   **cold**

Synonym means the same   **nice**   **kind**

🐆 Find the Opposite

Read these words. Draw a line to match each word to its opposite.

up	dry
inside	below
wet	down
above	outside
low	skinny
young	old
fat	high

short   **tall**

🐯 Opposite or the Same?

Look at these pictures and read the words. Are the words opposites, or do they mean the same thing? If the words are opposites, circle them. If the words mean the same thing, put a box around them.

friendly　angry　　jump　leap　　new　old

gift　present　　happy　sad　　big　huge

small　tiny　　asleep　awake

● How Quickly Can You Read?

These thermometers are playing opposites. Read these words as quickly as you can. How quickly do you think you can read them? Have your teacher time you as you read. Can you read the words faster a second time? Try it and see! Then check the temperature outside and write it on the thermometer.

mini
pizza
pull
full
bull
push
put
song
long
breath
worship
prophet
idea

idol
iron
heaven
heavy
only
altar
angel
tomato
potato
animal
message
tomorrow
argue

calf
half
aunt
palace

kiwi
ski
taxi

I read this page in: _____

Activity Time!

It's time to complete the activities for Chapter 27 in *God's Big Story* Level 1 workbook.

🦒 Sound Recognition

Look at this word. We've learned this one before. Do you remember what sound the O makes?

come

In *come*, the O is making a short U sound. It makes this sound in other words too. Read these words.

comfy   **command**   **nothing**

comfort   **coming**   **something**

Sometimes other sounds make the short U sound too. In these two words, the *-ou* is making a short U sound. Try to read these words. Remember that when *-le* comes at the end of a word, it says *ul*.

double

trouble

I have nothing in my pockets.

True or False?

Read these sentences. If a sentence says something that is true, write *true* in the blank. If the sentence says something that is not true, write *false* in the blank. Look carefully at the word *false*. It might not be spelled the way you think it should, so pay careful attention to how to write it properly.

true

false

A duck has three feet. _____

I can read words in my book. _____

My pizza will fly to the moon. _____

It is good to worship God. _____

📖 My First Bible Verses

God is more powerful than anything in heaven or on Earth. Nothing is too difficult for him. This Bible verse reminds us of that. God is speaking in this verse. He uses a long word. Sound this word out a little at a time.

an y thing   **anything**

Behold, I am the Lord, the God of all flesh. Is there anything too hard for Me?

Jeremiah 32:27

How Quickly Can You Read?

How quickly do you think you can read these words? Have your teacher time you as you read. Can you read the words faster a second time? Try it and see!

put	something	false	huge	musician
pull	only	anything	enjoy	measure
bull	fire	altar	toy	treasure
comfy	wire	confuse	destroy	pleasure
comfort	double	confusing	excuse	
command	trouble	puny	amuse	
coming	true			
nothing				

I read this page in: _____

It's Time to Read!
It's time to read Chapter 28 in *God's Big Story* Level 1.

🦒 Sound Recognition

You've learned that the letters -or say *-or* as in *orchid* or *store*. But sometimes these letters make a different sound, like in the word *sorry*. Sound out these words with our new -or sound.

sorry

sorrow

borrow

Dad, may I please borrow your book?

A Look at the Present Tense

Verbs tell us actions that are happening. Sometimes they tell us what already happened in the past. Sometimes they tell us things that will happen later in the future. And sometimes they tell us something that is happening right now.

When a verb tells us something that is happening right now, we call that a *present tense* verb. Read the sentences. Circle the word that shows what is happening; this is the verb. If the verb is telling us something that is happening right now, write P in the blank to show that this is a *present tense* verb.

Dad drove to the store yesterday. _____

Molly is riding her bike right now. _____

We will read a book tomorrow. _____

Matt is raking leaves in the yard. _____

Putting Things in Order

Read these words. Then put them in alphabetical order. If a word begins with A, put that word at the beginning of the list. Then look for a word that starts with B. Next, look for a word that starts with C. Use the alphabet to help you put the words in the correct order.

kangaroo _____

peacock _____

lion _____

dolphin _____

ox _____

monkey _____

snake _____

 How Quickly Can You Read?

These words have surrounded these animals. Can you read the words and set the animals free? Be careful that you don't get bitten! How quickly do you think you can read these words? Have your teacher time you as you read. Can you read the words faster a second time? Try it and see!

forever   rewrite   revisit   remind   resell   rename

reuse   refill   worth   sorry   sorrow   borrow

repay   destroy   comfy   comfort

worse   worst   work   word

something   command

anything   nothing

world   coming

joy   toy   worm

I read this page in: _____

Activity Time!

It's time to complete the activities for Chapter 28 in *God's Big Story* Level 1 workbook.

Let's Put It Together

Do you remember what a verb is? It's an action word that tells us what is happening. Sometimes verbs change their spelling when they are used in a sentence. Look at this word. See how it changes?

drive   **driving**   **drove**

These three words all come from the same word, but they're spelled differently. Verbs will often change forms (or spellings) to show us when something happened.

Here Comes Ing

One way verbs change is by adding -ing to the end of a word. Read these words. Then fill in the missing words.

jump + ing = *jumping*

walk + ing = *walking*

leap + ing = _____

read + ing = _____

listen + ing = _____

🐮 Let's Learn to Spell

Sometimes words change their spelling when we add -ing to the end. If a word ends in the letter E, that E will often drop off when we add -ing. Look at these words.

drive + ing = driving

live + ing = living

give + ing = giving

Read these words. Cross out the E on the end of each word. Then add -ing and write the new word in the blank.

Don't forget to cross out the E!

love + ing = _____

have + ing = _____

make + ing = _____

bake + ing = _____

serve + ing = _____

How Quickly Can You Read?

You read all these words in the last lesson. Do you think you can read them faster today? Have your teacher time you as you read. Can you read the words faster a second time? Try it and see!

comfy	joy	comfort	sorrow	enjoy	destroy
command	toy	sorry	borrow	remind	world
worth	rewrite			word	something
anything					forever
worse				never	revisit
worst					nothing
coming					resell
rename	refill	reuse		worm	work

Read it faster!

 I read this page in: _____

It's Time to Read!

It's time to read Chapter 29 in *God's Big Story* Level 1.

Sound Recognition

Here are some strange words that don't seem to follow the rules we've learned. Listen as your teacher reads the words. Then read them by yourself.

heart	**rough**
laugh	**enough**
tough	**cough**

A Look at Letters

Look at these three letters. You've seen them many times before. Usually these letters say *-eer* as in *fear* or *-er* as in *earth*. But in our new word below, they say *-ar* as in *heart*. Read these words. Then circle the letters -ear in each word.

ear	**heart**	
fear	**year**	**dear**
earth	**heard**	**search**

Find the Right Verb

Look at these pictures. Choose the correct verb from the box and write it in the blank. Then add -ing to the end of the verb. Read the sentences. Do they make sense?

drive	sing	laugh	cough

These ducklings are _____

The sick puppy _____

This is a _____ **donkey.**

My dog is _____ **the car.**

My First Bible Verses

Here's a new Bible verse for you to read.

Therefore comfort each other and edify one another, just as you also are doing.

1 Thessalonians 5:11

How Quickly Can You Read?

These dinosaurs have come to help you read. How quickly do you think you can read these words? Have your teacher time you as you read. Can you read the words faster a second time? Try it and see!

heart	laugh	cough	enough
among	honest	honor	prophet	who
honestly	does	hour	again	rough	promise
angel	friend	their	protect	pretty
heir	never	holy	provide	once
every	want	problem	else	four

 I read this page in: _____

Activity Time!

It's time to complete the activities for Chapter 29 in *God's Big Story* Level 1 workbook.

🦒 Sound Recognition

Here's a new sound to learn. When a word ends in the letters -ior, sometimes these letters say *yor* as in *savior*. Sound out these words one part at a time. Some of the words are tricky, so ask your teacher if you need help. Study the list until you can read it all by yourself.

A Viking warrior

savior	**senior**	**interior**	**superior**
junior	**warrior**	**exterior**	**behavior**

🐛 Let's Put It Together

Look at these words. You've learned some of them before. These words are called *contractions*. A contraction is made when two words are joined together to make one. Sound out the words.

did + not = didn't   **are + not = aren't**

is + not   = isn't   **do + not = don't**

has + not = hasn't

🦓 Who Took the Cookie?

Someone took a cookie and dropped crumbs all over the floor. Who was it? Read the clues to find out. Cross out the picture of each person who didn't take the cookie. Then circle the person who took it.

Grandmom and Grandpa don't like cookies.

Mommy said she didn't eat any cookies.

Daddy and sister Sally aren't at home, so they didn't take the cookie.

Who is left?

● How Quickly Can You Read?

Look at all the words surrounding this Viking warrior. Can you read them all? How quickly do you think you can read them? Have your teacher time you as you read. Can you read the words faster a second time? Try it and see! Then color the picture.

cough　　comfy　　command　　nothing

rough　　something　　earn　　trouble

laugh　　earth　　double　　altar　　only

heart　　behavior　　sorrow　　interior

superior　exterior　warrior　senior　sorry　false　true

junior　savior　borrow　fire　honor　honest　anything

I read this page in: _____

It's Time to Read!

It's time to read Chapter 30 in *God's Big Story* Level 1.

 Sound Recognition

When two vowels come together in a word, the first vowel says its name, and the second vowel is silent. You know how to sound out these words.

toe   **hoe**   **tiptoe**

But sometimes our vowels make different sounds. In these words, the letters -oe make an *-oo* sound.

shoe   **canoe**

Here are three other words with vowels that make strange sounds. Try to remember what these words look like so you'll know how to read them next time you see them.

woman

buy

guy

 # Fill in the Blank

Read the sentences. Choose the correct word from the box and write it in the blank.

| woman | canoe | buy | toe |

I left my shoe in the _____ at the river.

That _____ is my grandmother.

Did you hit your _____ on that stone?

Daddy, may we _____ some ice cream?

🦁 Let's Read Old English

Do you remember the Old English words we learned in Lesson 150? Two of the words were *thee* and *thou*. These words both mean *you*. Read these sentences in Old English. Draw a line from each sentence to the sentence that says the same thing in modern English. Use a blue crayon to circle the Old English words that are different than the English words you speak today. Then use a red crayon to circle the modern English words that mean the same thing as the Old English words you circled.

Matt, didst thou pick that rose?

Min has a pretty dress.

Min hath a pretty dress.

I will give you the rose to keep.

I will give thee the rose to keep.

Matt, did you pick that rose?

Thou hast a pretty rose.

🦏 How Quickly Can You Read?

Do you think these people speak Old English or modern English? What words would you use to speak to them? How quickly do you think you can read these words? Have your teacher time you as you read. Can you read the words faster a second time? Try it and see!

coin	rejoice	brought	heavy
coil	fought	caught	heaven
boil	thought	taught	shield
soil	ought	daughter	believe
noise	bought	slaughter	receive
moist	music	money	holy
choice	huge	honey	
voice	sought	desert	

 I read this page in: _____

Activity Time!

It's time to complete the activities for Chapter 30 in *God's Big Story* Level 1 workbook.

👧 Learning the Names of God

In the Bible, there are many names for God. This is because it's difficult to describe God with only one word. You know some of these words already. Try to sound out the other words. If you need help, ask your teacher.

God

Lord

Im man u el   **Immanuel**

That last word is a little tricky. *Immanuel* is a special name for God. This name means "God is with us." Another name you may have heard is the word *trinity*. This word means that there are three persons in God, but there is only one God. This is very difficult to understand. You'll learn more about this as you grow older, but right now you can read these words:

Trinity

God the Father

Jesus Christ

the Holy Spirit

A Look at Rhymes

It's fun to find words that rhyme. Read these words. Circle all the words that rhyme. If you find a word that doesn't rhyme with the other words, cross it out.

tries   copies   paper

wise   arise   advise

flies   baptize   skies

My First Bible Verses

Here's a new Bible verse for you to read. This verse uses the new name we learned for God.

"Behold, the virgin shall be with child, and bear a Son, and they shall call His name Immanuel," which is translated, "God with us."
Matthew 1:23

🦊 Fill in the Blank

Do you remember what a noun is? A noun names a person, place, or thing. Read the nouns in the box below. If the noun is a person, write the person in the first column. If the noun is a place, write the place in the second column. If the noun is a thing, write the thing in the third column.

daddy	Moses	Hannah	America
Texas	forest	grandmother	backyard
camel	door	pickle	Florida
hotdog	Africa	Henry	

person	**place**	**thing**

● How Quickly Can You Read?

These African animals have come to listen to you read. How quickly do you think you can read the words on this page? Have your teacher time you as you read. Can you read the words faster a second time? Try it and see!

Trinity	guy	behold	bear
God the Father	savior	beloved	pear
Jesus Christ	junior	count	thee
the Holy Spirit	senior	fount	clown
Immanuel	warrior	thine	eight
shoe	interior	bounce	sleigh
canoe	exterior	pounce	giraffe
woman			
buy			

I read this page in: _____

It's Time to Read!

It's time to read Chapter 31 in *God's Big Story* Level 1.

Sound Recognition

Look at these words and sound them out. Each of them ends with the letters -ain.

ain

stain   **contain**   **remain**

Sometimes these letters make a different sound when they come at the end of a word. Sometimes they will make the sound *-in* as in *certain*. Sound out these words.

captain   **certain**   **fountain**

curtain   **mountain**   **uncertain**

🐾 Fill in the Blank

Look at the pictures and read the sentences. Choose the correct word to complete each sentence. Write the word on the line.

Mommy _____
clean the stain out of my shirt.

couldn't   didn't   did

Captain Seagull _____
wearing any shoes.

is   isn't   almost

Let's walk up that tall
_____.

fountain   curtain   mountain

Putting Things in Order

Read these words. Some of the words might be difficult to pronounce, but you can use the pictures to help you. After you read the words, write them in alphabetical order. Remember to use the alphabet to help you put them in the correct order.

toucan

cheetah

owl

flamingo

sheep

pig

 How Quickly Can You Read?

How quickly do you think you can read these words? Have your teacher time you as you read. Can you read the words faster a second time? Try it and see!

stain	hasn't
contain	aren't
remain	alike
captain	agree
curtain	alive
certain	ashore
mountain	alone
fountain	hungry
uncertain	whistle
Trinity	why
God the Father	title
Jesus Christ	wrath
the Holy Spirit	wrist
Immanuel	sword

 I read this page in: _____

Activity Time!
It's time to complete the activities for Chapter 31 in *God's Big Story* Level 1 workbook.

🐾 Sound Recognition

Sometimes letters are silent and don't make any noise. In these words, the B is silent. Sound out the words, but don't sound out the B.

I like to eat the crumbs.

crumb	**bomb**
thumb	**debt**
numb	**plumber**
lamb	

Here are some more words with a silent B. These words have a long vowel sound.

climb

climbing

comb

combing

🦁 Find the Silent Sound

Read the story. Circle the words that have a silent B. Then draw a picture to show what the story is about.

Let's climb to the top of that mountain.

Do you see the flock of sheep grazing in the pasture?

Will the sheep play with the little lambs?

Here is a nice cobweb in the grass.

Let's Read Old English

This is a prayer from the Bible. But this prayer is written in Old English. Can you read it? There are two words with a silent B. Circle these words. Two other words are a little tricky. Try to sound them out before you read the prayer. If you need help, ask your teacher.

Our Father which art in heaven, **Hallowed** be Thy name.

Thy kingdom come, Thy will be done in earth, as it is in heaven.

Give us this day our daily bread.

And forgive us our debts, as we forgive our debtors.

And lead us not into **temptation**, but deliver us from evil:

For thine is the kingdom, and the power, and the glory, for ever. Amen.

Matthew 6:9-13

🐨 How Quickly Can You Read?

These koalas love to climb, but it's easier when words are not in their way! How quickly do you think you can read these words? Have your teacher time you as you read. Can you read the words faster a second time? Try it and see!

crumb	climb	nothing
thumb	climbed	something
numb	climbing	alone
lamb	comb	only
bomb	combed	double
bombing	sword	trouble
bombed	comfy	hungry
debt	mountain	true
debtor	command	false
plumber	angel	anything
plumbing	coming	

I read this page in: _____

I ate a bowlful!

 # Sound Recognition

Sometimes we add something to the end of a word to change the word. When we do this, the letters we add are called a *suffix*. Look at these three letters. They say *full*. These letters are a suffix that we can add to many words. Sound out the words below.

ful

cupful	**sinful**	**playful**	**powerful**
joyful	**fearful**	**careful**	**spoonful**

Solve the Riddle

Here is a riddle for you to solve. Read the riddle. Then choose the correct answer and write it in the blank.

A houseful, a hole full,
But you cannot gather a bowlful.

What is it? _____

water   dust   smoke

Fill in the Blank

Choose the correct word from the box to complete each sentence.

colorful	cheerful	careful

My baby sister is a _____ baby.

This is a _____ rainbow.

Be _____ with that sharp knife.

How Quickly Can You Read?

Here's a pageful of toys. Can you read the words around them? How quickly do you think you can read these words? Have your teacher time you as you read. Can you read the words faster a second time? Try it and see!

colorful   cupful   joyful

head   faithful   mouthful

spoonful   fearful   sinful   lamb

powerful   thoughtful  cheerful   mountain

thumb   careful   bombing   thankful

numb   crumb   bomb   bread   candy   playful

 penny   bombed   graceful

empty   tempt   thread

 I read this page in: _____

Lesson 162

🐾 Sound Recognition

Here's a new suffix for us to learn. A suffix is a group of letters added to the end of a word. We add this suffix to the end of a word to change the word. Read these words.

sickness

ness

sickness	**illness**
sadness	**neatness**
wellness	**kindness**

Sometimes a word will look a little differently when we add a suffix. Read these words. Then see how they change when we add the suffix *-ness*.

lazy	laziness
holy	holiness
salty	saltiness
icy	iciness

laziness

🐵 Let's Put It Together

Did you know that we can add more than one suffix to the end of a word? Read these words. Then add the suffix *-ness* to the end of each word to make a new word.

careful + ness = carefulness

faithful + ness = _____

joyful + ness = _____

helpful + ness = _____

powerful + ness = _____

Let's Draw a Picture

Choose one of the words below and draw a picture to show what the word means.

sadness

slowness

happiness

playfulness

My First Bible Verses

Here's a new Bible verse for you to read.

I would have lost heart, unless I had believed that I would see the goodness of the Lord in the land of the living.

Psalm 27:13

🦏 How Quickly Can You Read?

Look at all these lazy sloths! Can you read the words before the sloths decide to get up from their naps? How quickly do you think you can read these words? Have your teacher time you as you read. Can you read the words faster a second time? Try it and see!

slowness   isn't   illness   sadness   sickness

kindness   softness   wetness   wellness

goodness   neatness   laziness   weakness

faithfulness   happiness   saltiness   holiness

playfulness   should   could   joyfulness

shouldn't   would   helpfulness   carefulness

powerfulness   gratefulness   iciness   wouldn't   couldn't

I read this page in: _____

Activity Time!

It's time to complete the activities for Chapter 32 in *God's Big Story* Level 1 workbook.

🐱 Let's Put It Together

When we add a prefix or a suffix to a word, it makes a new word. If we take the prefix or suffix away, we will have the same word as we had at first. This word is called a *root word*. A root word is a word without any prefix or suffix added to it.

playful

Read these words. Cross out all the suffixes. Then write what is left in the blank. The first one is done for you.

Word	Root Word
fear~~ful~~	fear
playful	
goodness	
careful	
spoonful	
softness	

🐆 Find the Match

Read the words. Draw a line to match each word to the correct picture.

sadness

happiness

angriness

🦓 A Look at Contractions

Do you remember what a contraction is? A *contraction* is made when two words are joined together to make one word. When these words are joined together, we leave out the O. Then we write an apostrophe in the O's place. Read the words. Then write the contraction on the line. The first two words are done for you.

did + not   =   **didn't**

would + not   =   **wouldn't**

is + not   =   _____

has + not   =   _____

could + not   =   _____

should + not =   _____

🐀 How Quickly Can You Read?

Look at all this ice cream! Read the words on the page. When you find the words *ice cream*, color them red. How quickly do you think you can read these words? Have your teacher time you as you read. Can you read the words faster a second time? Try it and see!

rough	honor	four	who	their
enough	honest	ghost	heir	holy
heart	among	pretty	every	feeling
laugh	does	once	never	healing
tough	hour	honestly	friend	walking
cough	again	ice cream	want	talking

 I read this page in: _____

It's Time to Read!

It's time to read Chapter 33 in *God's Big Story* Level 1.

Sound Recognition

I am a scientist

Sometimes the letter C will be silent in a word. Look at these three letters. When they come together in a word, the letter C will be silent. Sound out these words.

sci

scissors   **scientist**

science   **disciple**   **fascinate**

 ## Find the Silent Letters

Read the words. Each of these words has one silent letter in it. Circle the silent letter in each word.

scissors   **scientist**   **fascinate**

thumb   **plumber**   **lamb**

plumbing   **disciple**   **bomb**

science   **debt**

🐻 Find the Silent Letters

Read the words on this sign. If a word is a noun, circle it. If a word isn't a noun, cross it out.

disciple   cat   were
scissors   is   Matt   the
dolphin   bomb   lamb

📖 My First Bible Verses

Here's a new Bible verse for you to read. In this verse, Jesus is speaking to His disciples, the people who followed and obeyed Him. Are you a disciple of Jesus?

"By this all will know that you are My disciples, if you have love for one another."
John 13:35

 How Quickly Can You Read?

How quickly do you think you can read these words? Have your teacher time you as you read. Can you read the words faster a second time? Try it and see!

scientist	the Holy Spirit	junior
fascinate	Immanuel	senior
scissors	shoe	warrior
disciple	canoe	interior
science	woman	exterior
Trinity	buy	superior
God the Father	guy	behavior
Jesus Christ	savior	

 I read this page in: _____

Activity Time!

It's time to complete the activities for Chapter 33 in *God's Big Story* Level 1 workbook.

🐘 Let's Review

We've learned all the sounds in these words. Read the words as quickly as you can. If you miss a word, circle it. When you've read all the words, go back and read the ones you missed.

table	peddle
cable	toddler
noble	ladle
wobble	cradle
nibble	purple
bumblebee	simple
puddle	people
kindle	couple

example

disciple

Let's Make a Sentence

Look at the picture. Choose a word from the box and write a sentence about the picture. Ask your teacher if you need help spelling a word in your sentence.

table	bumblebee	puddle
wobble	cradle	purple

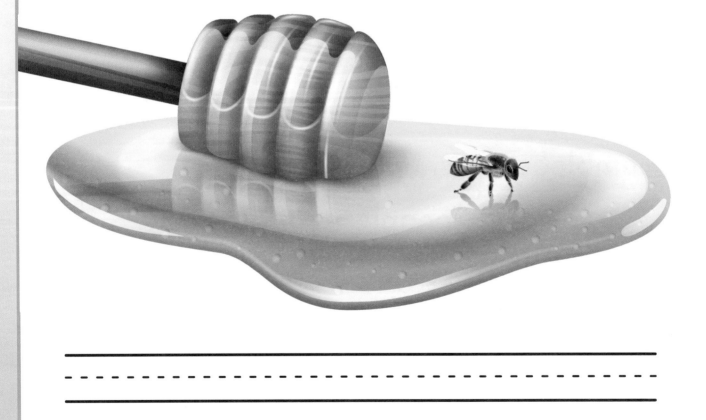

Working with Suffixes

Read these words. Then add a suffix to the end of each word to make a new word. Be careful! If the word ends in a Y, change the Y to an I before you add the suffix.

kind + ness = kindness

good + ness = _____

mouth + ful = _____

salty + ness = _____

happy + ness = _____

 Let's Draw a Picture

Read the sentences. Choose one of the sentences and draw a picture to show what is happening in the sentence.

The pot is boiling on the stove.

Matt likes to make paper airplanes.

Heather will color the picture of the heart red.

🐭 How Quickly Can You Read?

How quickly do you think you can read these words? Have your teacher time you as you read. Can you read the words faster a second time? Try it and see!

tired	hurt	learn	tough	knight
hired	nurse	heard	angel	knuckle
fired	purse	search	knit	know
expired	curse	yearn	knitting	known
turn	earth	heart	knee	knowing
lurk	earn	laugh	knelt	

I read this page in: _____

It's Time to Read!

It's time to read Chapter 34 in *God's Big Story* Level 1.

Sound Recognition

You've seen these words before. Sound them out.

> Quack, quack!

quack   **quick**   **queen**

quiz   **quite**   **question**

Sometimes -qu makes a different sound. In some words, it will make a *-ck* sound. Listen as your teacher reads these words. Then read them by yourself.

quart   **quarter**

a quart
of milk

Try to remember how these words look so you won't need to sound them out next time you see them.

Here are some other sight words to learn. Listen as your teacher reads them. We've seen some of these words before. Do you remember them? Read the words. Then read the sentence.

been   **guard**

though **already**

build

I've already been to the zoo.

Find the Match

Read the sentences. Draw a line to match each sentence with the correct picture.

The carpenter will build a house.

The little boy has one quarter.

Mommy has already been to the grocery store.

🐾 Fill in the Blank

Do you remember what a noun is? A noun names a person, place, or thing. Read the nouns in the box below. If the noun is a person, write the person in the first column. If the noun is a place, write the place in the second column. If the noun is a thing, write the thing in the third column.

doctor	fireman	farmer	church
farm	Alabama	nurse	crumb
truck	kangaroo	stairs	Iceland
Bible	zoo	policeman	

Person	Place	Thing

🦏 How Quickly Can You Read?

This carpenter is building a house, and these words have come to watch. How quickly do you think you can read them all? Have your teacher time you as you read. Can you read the words faster a second time? Try it and see!

been   allow   played   should   quarter   worm

agree   looked   though   people   lasted   away

would   work   could   closed

awake   example

world   jumped

word   disciple

across   scientist

talked   already   scissors   worst

build   guard   science   fascinate   quart

I read this page in: _____

Activity Time!

It's time to complete the activities for Chapter 34 in *God's Big Story* Level 1 workbook.

Sound Recognition

Listen as your teacher reads these words. Pay attention to how the ending letters sound. Then read the words by yourself.

ious

curious   **previous**   **religious**

serious   **obvious**

Sometimes this ending has a *-sh* sound. Listen as your teacher reads these words. Then read them by yourself.

precious

ferocious

delicious

anxious

cautious

The bird is curious.

🦝 Fill in the Blank

Read the sentences. Choose the correct word from the box and write it in the blank.

delicious	precious	ferocious

The Bible is a _____ gift from God.

A lion is a _____ beast.

This cupcake is _____ !

Finish the Sentence

Choose the correct words to finish the sentence. Then color the picture.

Min has four _____ **of fresh** _____ .

quarts   quarters   mil   milk

🐹 How Quickly Can You Read?

How quickly do you think you can read these words? Have your teacher time you as you read. Can you read the words faster a second time? Try it and see!

delicious	serious	guard	session
precious	obvious	untrue	tension
ferocious	previous	unchain	niece
anxious	anything	unloved	grief
cautious	understand	unknown	field
religious	powerful	version	believe
curious	punishment	mission	receive
		passion	ceiling

 I read this page in: _____

It's Time to Read!

It's time to read Chapter 35 in *God's Big Story* Level 1.

Sound Recognition

Do you remember our silent B words?
Sound out these words.

crumb	**debt**
thumb	**climb**
lamb	**comb**
bomb	

The turtle has a green thumb.

Some silent B words have an *-oo* sound. Listen as your teacher reads these words. Then read them by yourself.

womb   **tomb**

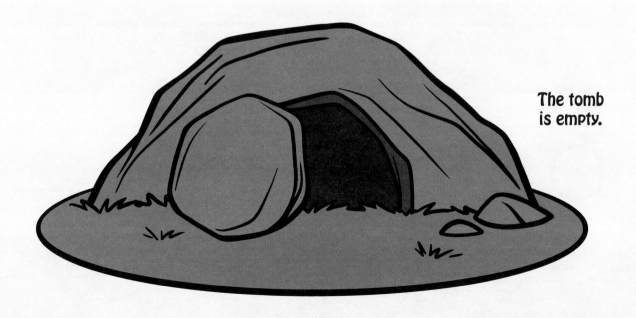

The tomb is empty.

Putting Things in Order

Read these words. Some of the words might be difficult to pronounce, but you can use the pictures to help you. After you read the words, write them in alphabetical order. Remember to use the alphabet to help you put them in the correct order.

banana
_____

mushroom
_____

tomato
_____

apple
_____

potato
_____

orange
_____

carrot
_____

Let's Put It Together

Read the words. If the word has a long O sound, color the word green. If the word has an -oo sound, color it blue.

comb	**zoom**
tomb	**dome**
room	**womb**
home	**honeycomb**

How Quickly Can You Read?

Can you help these fruits and vegetables read these words? How quickly do you think you can read the words? Have your teacher time you as you read. Be careful! Some of these words are tricky. Can you read them faster a second time? Try it and see!

zoom	anything	guard	clown
dome	someone	loud	crowded
tomb	powerful	crowd	mushroom
comb	playfulness	wow	pepperoni
room	else	count	safari
home	who	bounce	pizza
womb	want	pounce	zucchini
climb	friend	down	potato

 I read this page in: _____

Activity Time!

It's time to complete the activities for Chapter 35 in *God's Big Story* Level 1 workbook.

🦓 A Look at Contractions

Do you remember what a contraction is? A contraction is made when two words are joined together to make one. When two words are joined together, we usually leave out an O. But sometimes we leave out other letters. Read these words and their contractions.

We'll all have ice cream!

did + not = didn't

is + not = isn't

we + have = we've

they + have = they've

we + will = we'll

they + will = they'll

will + not = won't

🐹 Fix the Sentence

Read the sentences. Add the correct punctuation to the end of each sentence. Then look for any contractions. If you find a contraction, add an apostrophe to the word where it needs one. Then color the picture.

. **period**

? **question mark**

! **exclamation point**

' **apostrophe**

Remember, if the sentence is making a statement or telling about something that happened, it probably ends with a period. If the sentence is asking a question, it will end with a question mark. If something very exciting or scary happens in the sentence, it might end with an exclamation point.

Is my friend coming to see me

I think we ll play a game if he comes

I don t think you remember my friend's name

Won t you come play with Dickie and me

Let's Make a Match

Draw a line to match each contraction with the correct words.

they'll	we will
didn't	will not
hasn't	they have
won't	they will
we've	we have
they've	did not
we'll	has not

🦏 How Quickly Can You Read?

Here's a new word to learn. Try to sound it out by yourself. Then read the rest of the words on the page. How quickly do you think you can read them? Have your teacher time you as you read. Can you read the words faster a second time? Try it and see!

soldier

didn't	bread	crowd	womb	before
we've	head	shout	tomb	friend
they've	dead	soldiers	guard	phone
we'll	leather	bedtime	himself	phonics
they'll	heaven	sunshine	someone	Joseph
won't	loud	snowball	sometimes	brother

 I read this page in: _____

It's Time to Read!

It's time to read Chapter 36 in *God's Big Story* Level 1.

Proper Nouns

Do you remember what a noun is? It names a person, place, or thing. One type of noun is called a *proper noun*. A proper noun is a word that gives us the name of a special person, place, or thing.

There are many days in the week, but there is only one Sunday. Sunday is a proper noun because it is a specific day. There are many months in the year, but there is only one month of June. June and all the other names of months are proper nouns.

We can read about lots of people, but when we read about Moses, we are reading about a specific or a special person. Moses is a proper noun because it is talking about one particular person. All names of specific people are proper nouns.

Read these proper nouns.

Moses	Texas	Monday
Elijah	Alaska	July
David	Florida	Wednesday
Jesus	Tennessee	December

🐾 Fix the Sentence

All proper nouns will begin with a capital letter. Look at the proper nouns in the columns above. They all start with a capital letter.

In these sentences, someone forgot to capitalize the first letters of each sentence. They forgot to capitalize the proper nouns too. Can you fix this mess? If a letter is supposed to be capitalized, cross it out and write the capital letter above it.

we went to texas yesterday.

min feeds the chickens on monday.

was david the king of israel?

my brother sam mows the yard on friday.

🦁 Let's Read a Story

Here are two stories that Jesus told about the kingdom of heaven. Read the stories. Then draw a picture of one of the stories. (You can read these stories in the Bible in Matthew 13:44-46.) There are some new words in this story. Try to sound out these words on your own. If you need help, ask your teacher.

beautiful   pearl

What Is the Kingdom of Heaven Like?

The kingdom of heaven is like treasure hidden in a field. And a man found it and hid it. And he is filled with joy, and he goes and sells all that he has and buys that field.

Again, the kingdom of heaven is like a merchant seeking beautiful pearls. When he had found one pearl of great price, he went and sold all that he had and bought the pearl.

How Quickly Can You Read?

Pete the Parrot has decided to go hunting for treasure. Can you help him by reading these words? How quickly do you think you can read them all? Have your teacher time you as you read. Can you read the words faster a second time? Try it and see!

precious	more	tonight
delicious	anything	alright
soldier	anywhere	delight
angel	anymore	eight
heaven	behind	sleigh
death	before	weigh
dead	become	brought
worship	became	caught
empty	believe	taught
thing	higher	daughter
where	mighty	

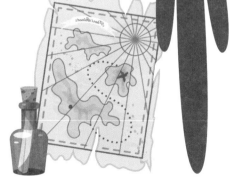

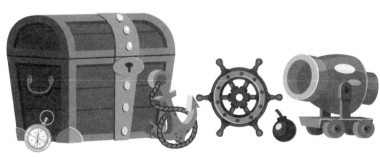

I read this page in: _____

🐻 Common Nouns

A noun names a person, place, or thing. A proper noun is a word that gives us the name of a particular or special person, place, or thing.

Another kind of noun is called a *common noun*. Common nouns tell us the name of something, but they don't tell us the name of a specific thing. *Dog* is a common noun because it doesn't tell us which specific dog we're talking about. *Church* is a common noun because it doesn't tell us which church we're talking about. Read these common nouns.

day	**dog**	**brother**
hat	**field**	**church**

Which hat is yours?

🐆 Let's Make a Match

Look at the first column of words. These words are all common nouns. They don't tell us which particular person or place they're talking about. Draw a line from each common noun to a proper noun that matches it.

day   Vermont

mouse   Tuesday

uncle   Uncle Bob

state   Min the Mouse

🐱 Find the Proper Noun

Read the sentences. Fill in the blank with a proper noun. Remember to capitalize all proper nouns.

My name is _____ .

The day of the week today is _____ .

My home state is _____ .

My church is called _____ .

 Common or Proper Noun?

Read these words as quickly as you can. Then choose two colors. Color all the proper nouns one color, and color all the common nouns another color. Have your teacher time you as you read the words. Can you read the words faster a second time? Try it and see!

Idaho	Peter	giant	pasture
disciple	Thursday	mother	nature
angel	Heather	July	September
tree	holiday	guard	mountain
Adam	picnic	rocket	soldier
woman	giraffe	zucchini	Jesus Christ
God	Christmas	August	
daughter	pizza	Sally	

 I read this page in: _____

Activity Time!

It's time to complete the activities for Chapter 36 in *God's Big Story* Level 1 workbook.

Lesson 172

Find the Synonym

Do you remember learning about antonyms and synonyms? If two words mean opposite things, we call those words *antonyms*. If two words mean the same or almost the same thing, we call them *synonyms*. Read the words. Draw a line to match each word to its synonym.

a lot of   many

large

little

keep

sick

leap

begin

angry

mad

small

start

jump

big

ill

save

🐆 Find the Opposite

Read the sentences. Find a word in the box that is the opposite of the word in bold. This is an antonym. Write the antonym on the line. Does this change what the sentence means?

alone   together

| close | white | loud | wet | up |

You are **quiet** this morning. _____

We've already walked **down** the stairs. _____

I have a pretty **black** cat. _____

Would you please **open** _____
the door, Sammy? _____

The grass was **dry** _____
when the soldiers came. _____

🦁 Let's Draw a Picture

Can you think of two words that are opposites or antonyms? Write the words in the blanks. Then draw a picture to show how these words are opposites.

_____   _____

Clean   **Dirty**   **Inside**   **Outside**

⬤ How Quickly Can You Read?

These frogs have decided to sing you a song while you read these words. Can you sing the words as you read them? How quickly do you think you can do it? Have your teacher time you as you read. Can you read the words faster a second time? Try it and see!

thing	angel	behind	higher
where	heaven	before	mighty
more	death	become	tonight
anything	dead	became	alright
anywhere	eight	believe	delight
anymore	sleigh		
worship	weigh		
empty	brought		
precious	caught		
delicious	taught		
soldier	daughter		

 I read this page in: _____

It's Time to Read!

It's time to read Chapter 37 in *God's Big Story* Level 1.

Sound Recognition

We've learned how to sound out these words. Read them quickly.

true   **blue**   **clue**   **unglue**

Some words end with these same letters, but they make a different sound. You've seen one of these words before. Can you sound them out? Ask your teacher to give you a clue if you need help.

argue   **rescue**   **issue**   **statue**

value   **continue**   **tissue**

Changing Verbs

The verbs are missing from these sentences. Under each blank, you'll find a verb. Write the verb in the blank and add -ed to the end of it. Then read the sentence. Does it make sense? Be careful! If a verb ends in the letter E, you only need to add the letter D to the end. The first sentence is done for you.

The children **argued** over the toy.
argue + ed

The boy and girl _____ the kitten.
rescue + ed

We _____ to read until bedtime.
continue + ed

What _____ to the fish?
happen + ed

I _____ wash the dishes.
help + ed

Putting Things in Order

Matt and Min are taking a canoe trip through the forest. They've seen many things along the river. Can you make a list of the things they've seen? Write the words in alphabetical order. Remember to use the alphabet to help you put the words in the correct order.

ladybug	hedgehog	owl	fox
deer	rabbit	butterfly	

_____   _____

_____   _____

_____   _____

_____

_____

🦏 How Quickly Can You Read?

Matt and Min found many creatures in the forest. These creatures have come to listen to you read. How quickly do you think you can read these words? Have your teacher time you as you read. Can you read the words faster a second time? Try it and see!

argue	we'll	greatness	commanded
value	they'll	mightiness	rescued
rescue	won't	father	continued
continue	soldier	gather	happened
issue	length	mother	said
tissue	strength	brother	was
statue	powerful	nation	picture
we've	faithful	obey	Scripture
they've	faithfulness	obeyed	capture

 I read this page in: _____

Activity Time!

It's time to complete the activities for Chapter 37 in *God's Big Story* Level 1 workbook.

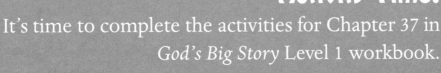

🐑 Let's Put It Together

Do you remember what a prefix is? A prefix is something that comes at the beginning of a word. A prefix will change a word's meaning. Here's a new prefix. This prefix means *wrong*. Let's add this to a word and see what happens. Sound out these words.

mis + match = mismatch

mistake   **mislay**

misfit   **misuse**

misjudge   **misspent**

mismatched socks

🐛 Which Prefix?

Read these words. Choose the correct prefix to add to each word to make a new word. Be careful! Read your word after you're finished to be sure it's a real word.

mis   **dis**

_____obey   _____cover

_____judge   _____take

_____fit   _____honor

_____agree   _____match

🦓 Contractions Review

Read the words. Write the correct contraction on the line. Don't forget to add an apostrophe. The first two are done for you.

is + not = isn't

would + not = wouldn't

has + not = _____

we + will = _____

will + not = _____

they + have = _____

they + will = _____

we + have = _____

did + not = _____

How Quickly Can You Read?

These birds have come to learn about prefixes. Read the words. Then circle all the words that have a *mis-* or *dis-* prefix. How quickly do you think you can read them? Have your teacher time you as you read. Then color the birds.

mislay	misuse	gather	continued
dishonor	misspent	mother	happened
disunity	distrust	obey	Scripture
strength	faithfulness	obeyed	capture
powerful	greatness	commanded	mismatch
faithful	disagree	misfit	mistake
disloyal	discover	misjudge	
mightiness	father	rescued	

 I read this page in: _____

It's Time to Read!

It's time to read Chapter 38 in *God's Big Story* Level 1.

Sound Recognition

Look at these three letters. Usually, they say *age* as in *page* or *rage*.
But sometimes these letters say *-idj*. Sound out these words with our
new sound.

age

image	**message**
package	**cottage**
baggage	**language**

This is a special message for you.

🐵 Let's Put It Together

Do you remember what the plural form of a word is? *Plural* means a word that is talking about more than one thing. If we have one dog, we say *dog*. But if we have more than one dog, we add an S to the end of the word and say *dogs*. Sometimes words change how they are spelled when we make them plural. Sometimes a Y will change to an I, and sometimes an F will change to a V. We learned about this in Lesson 115 and Lesson 135. Read these words. Add an ending to each word to make it plural. The first few are done for you.

penny   pennies

sky   skies

wife   wives

baby   _____

bunny   _____

city   _____

candy   _____

knife   _____

loaf   _____

"I will guard my pennies!"

🐾 Let's Make a Match

Read the words. Draw a line to match each word with its meaning.

image   a small house

                               the words you speak

baggage
                               a suitcase or
                               something you pack

garbage
                               a picture of
                               something

cottage
                               trash that needs to
language   be thrown away

Stop the
garbage thief!

🐇 How Quickly Can You Read?

These words look like they're ready for something sweet to eat. How quickly do you think you can read these words? Have your teacher time you as you read. Can you read the words faster a second time? Try it and see!

image	average	away	young
damage	message	about	coming
manage	cottage	amaze	nothing
savage	garbage	again	something
voyage	postage	put	only
package	luggage	push	fire
baggage	language	bush	together
sausage	arise	many	double
	surprise	any	trouble

 I read this page in: _____

Activity Time!

It's time to complete the activities for Chapter 38 in *God's Big Story* Level 1 workbook.

🐘 Sight Words

Here are some new words to learn. You may have seen some of them before. These words don't sound the way we think they should. Listen as your teacher reads them. Then read them by yourself.

wonder   **month**   **aunt**

country   **favorite**

How many countries are there on Earth?

🐱 Fill in the Blank

Read the sentences. Fill in the blank with the correct word. Be careful! Check to be sure that the word is spelled correctly.

I _____ how many stars are in the sky.

wunder   wonder

February is a short _____ .

month   munth

How big is the _____ of Spain?

country   cuntry

My _____ pie is pumpkin pie.

favrit   favorite

Billy gave some flowers to his _____ .

ant   aunt

Let's Make a Match

Write the name for each number in the spaces below. If you need help with spelling, look on the crab's sign.

1 _____   6 _____

2 _____   7 _____

3 _____   8 _____

4 _____   9 _____

5 _____   10 _____

one   four   eight
two   six   ten   nine
seven   five   three

How Quickly Can You Read?

You read most of these words in the last lesson. Do you think you can read them faster today? Have your teacher time you as you read. Check to see if you read them faster than you did in the last lesson. Can you read the words even faster a second time? Try it and see!

country	savage	arise	again	young
wonder	average	amaze	quake	together
favorite	message	put	coming	bush
aunt	luggage	push	nothing	double
month	language	surprise	trouble	something
image	cottage	away	many	only
garbage	postage	about	any	

I read this page in: _____

It's Time to Read!

It's time to read Chapter 39 in *God's Big Story* Level 1.

🦓 Let's Look at Numbers

We use numbers every day. Sometimes we use the numbers one, two, and three. But sometimes we use different words for numbers. Read these words. These are called *ordinal numbers*.

first	**sixth**
second	**seventh**
third	**eighth**
fourth	**ninth**
fifth	**tenth**

🐱 A Place in Line

Let's use our ordinal numbers in a sentence. Look at this line of animals. The goat is first in line. Which animal comes next? Write the correct number to complete each sentence. If you need help with spelling, look at the list above. The first two are done for you.

The goat is **first** in line.

The rabbit is **fourth** in line.

The turkey is _____ in line.

The cow is _____ in line.

The dog is _____ in line.

The sheep is _____ in line.

The horse is _____ in line.

The chick is _____ in line.

Adding a Suffix

Read the words. Add the suffix -ful to the end of each word. Read the word again. Is it a real word? If the word isn't a real word after you add the suffix, cross it out.

cup + ful   =   cupful

fear + ful   =   _____

glad + ful   =   _____

joy + ful   =   _____

silly + ful   =   _____

care + ful   =   _____

power + ful   =   _____

"I need a
cupful of flour."

How Quickly Can You Read?

These animals are all walking in a line, just like the ordinal numbers we learned. How quickly do you think you can read each line of words? Have your teacher time you as you read. Can you read the words faster a second time? Try it and see!

seventh	tenth	Philip	gentle
fifth	ninth	Joseph	wage
first	prison	phone	urgent
third	risen	graph	huge
second	famine	agent	bridge
eighth	quake	Ralph	
fourth	children	angel	
sixth	phonics	germ	

I read this page in: _____

Activity Time!

It's time to complete the activities for Chapter 39 in *God's Big Story* Level 1 workbook.

Let's Put It Together

Look at these words. You've seen them before. Sound them out as quickly as you can.

my	**our**	**her**	**them**
your	**it**	**him**	

These are words that talk about me and you and other people. Sometimes we add an ending to these words to change them. Can you read these words quickly with their endings?

myself   **herself**

yourself   **himself**

itself   **themselves**

ourselves

When we read, these words tell us what kind of person we're reading about.

I read my book by myself.